Celebrating Christmas

An Anthology of

Tales, Tips, and Truths about Christmas

Parson's Creek Press©
Discovering Truth Is A Wise Use Of Time;
Applying Truth To Oneself Is Obedience;
Teaching Truth To Others Is Compassion.©

COMPILED BY

MARGERY KISBY WARDER

Celebrating Christmas
An Anthology of Tales, Tips, and Truths about Christmas
©Margery Kisby Warder, November 15, 2017
All rights reserved.

Cover Design: Margery Kisby Warder
Dreamstime and Pixabay are great resources for self-pubishing authors.

Format Design: Margery Kisby Warder & CreateSpace

Published by Parson's Creek Press©

Parson's Creek Press© is the copyrighted logo for a virtual publishing company that almost always uses CreateSpace for original writing by Margery or Paul Warder or by non-paid contributing writers whose writing meets the standards held by Parson's Creek Press©. Parson's Creek Press© mission statement: Bringing Inspirational Characters & Writing to Readers of All Ages Because Good Words Can Lead to Good Works©.

Scripture quotations marked "KJV" are taken from the Holy Bible, King James Version (Public Domain).

Scripture quotations marked (CEV) are from the Contemporary English Version Copyright © 1991, 1992, 1995 by American Bible Society, Used by Permission.

Scriptures marked RSV are taken from the REVISED STANDARD VERSION (RSV): Scripture taken from the REVISED STANDARD VERSION, Grand Rapids: Zondervan, 1971.

Scripture quotations marked (NIV) are taken from the Holy Bible, New International Version®, NIV®. Copyright © 1973, 1978, 1984, 2011 by Biblica, Inc.™ Used by permission of Zondervan. All rights reserved worldwide. **www.zondervan.com** The "NIV" and "New International Version" are trademarks registered in the United States Patent and Trademark Office by Biblica, Inc.™

Scriptures marked TLB are taken from the THE LIVING BIBLE (TLB): Scripture taken from THE LIVING BIBLE copyright© 1971. Used by permission of Tyndale House Publishers, Inc., Carol Stream, Illinois 60188. All rights reserved.

Scripture quotations taken from the New American Standard Bible® (NASB), Copyright © 1960, 1962, 1963, 1968, 1971, 1972, 1973, 1975, 1977, 1995 by The Lockman Foundation Used by permission. www.Lockman.org

November 2017
All rights reserved.

ISBN:13:978-1979717168
ISBN-10:1979717168

Dedication

To Everyone Who Celebrates Christmas
Whether with someone or alone
Who, when evening or morning comes
Wants Christ to feel at home.

ANTHOLOGY COMPILED BY MARGERY KISBY WARDER

TABLE OF CONTENTS

RECIPES

HOTLINKS FOR MORE CHRISTMAS BLESSINGS

BIOGRAPHIES OF AUTHORS

ABOUT THE ANTHOLOGY EDITOR/COMPILER

Thank You from Margery Kisby Warder

As the principle organizer for this compilation, I want to thank each individual who came to our workshops or sent me her or his writing about Christmas so it could be a part of this anthological publication. You were great to get to know and I hope we will do similar work together in the future. I pray your Christmases, and all the days before and after them, will be a little brighter because you creatively stepped beyond your comfort zones to share your lives with others.

My second huge *thank you* goes to my husband who still, even after seeing the morningside of midnight, is willing to write with me. I've heard the long-marrieds say wallpapering or remodeling can test a marriage, but I'm guessing you'd say a hearty *Amen* to the gentleman who claimed he discovered there's really only room for one writer in a house. I sincerely thank you, My Man, for supporting my writing efforts and for accompanying me to writer events. I thank the Lord that I get to do life with you.

As the compiling editor who studied Kathy Ide's proofreading book only to marvel at how rules change, I strongly hope each of the nearly three thousand seven hundred little surviving commas rests where it does the most good for the eyes that see the comma. I campaigned to have every typo serve time somewhere besides in this book, but I've read long enough to know typos have a way of sneaking in undetected, sometimes right under our noses for years. I suppose everyone who pushes "publish" knows to err is almost guaranteed and prays readers remember we're all fallible. That said, I offer another huge *thank you* to the courageous ones who spent hours hunting for mistakes–especially my husband Paul and to the gals around the proofing tables: Anna Lisa, Beverly, Dianne, Fran, Jane, Marilyn, and Sybil. You are each deeply appreciated by the careful readers and me.

Margery Kisby Warder

Margerywarder@gmail.com

https://www.amazon.com/Margery-Kisby-Warder/e/B00GPELE7I

Merry Christmas, Reader

Thank you for securing a copy of this anthology. We contributors wrote about Christmas with you in mind. You have been prayed over, precious reader, and it is our desire that what you read here will bless you. Our prayer is that the Christ of Christmas will forever be a part, not only of Christmas, but of your life forever. We all wish you a very nice Christmas.

Readers of anthologies sometimes discover a new writer to follow. Several of us have, or will have in the future, other writing available for readers. Please see the brief biograhies on the last pages to discover more of our writings and how to follow us.

A friendly reminder: When you do find an author you like, a couple online words about a book can encourage us and help others learn of our writing. Thank you in advance. Most of our books can be found on Amazon.

Anthology Contributors, November, 2017

Nonfiction

The fear of the Lord is the beginning of knowledge;

but fools despise wisdom and instruction.

Psalm 1:7 (KJV)

1 ~ CHRISTMAS WITHOUT PERFECTION

LORI KLICKMAN

Although I still have a few Thanksgiving leftovers in the fridge, my tree is up, my house is decorated, and I've made my list of Christmas cookies to bake...SO that means it's officially the Christmas season. For the most part, that's a wonderful thing, but with all the wonder comes a bit of weary as well.

One thing in life I have noticed is that there are those who are partygoers and those of us who are party-throwers. Some are thermometers; others are thermostats. Givers and receivers. One category is not better than the other. The truth is, both are needed for a fulfilling experience. And no matter what side of the fence you're on, Christmas can be exhausting.

I am more content throwing the party. (I'm pretty sure it's a control issue under the guise of servanthood - now, there's something to chew on.) I recognize that God has given me a gift, an ability to make things "special." I know it's a gift from God because it brings me so much joy and satisfaction when I use it.

Then there's that other voice...Do you ever hear it? Shhhh, listen:

"Oh my gosh, why do YOU have to do EVERYTHING? Must be nice

tobe invited to parties, just eat the cookies, instead of making them, sit downto a beautiful table, with courses of stunning food and three desserts, sit in the ambiance of twinkling lights and the warmth and comfort of a beautifully decorated home, get uniquely wrapped gifts that someone had to put tons of effort into finding, shipping. Oh - don't forget the stocking stuffers. You think it's easy to creatively fill a stocking with little items you might actually like? Do others even REALIZE how much time, effort, and energy goes into making THEIR holiday special? Oh, poor child, you must be exhausted - not that anyone cares, or wants to help."

I hate that voice. And trust me, I know the depths from which it heralds. God gives. The devil comes to steal and destroy. When I sit down to coffee with that voice, things get ugly. I go into "martyr-mode" and anyone near me will either be shamed (I can easily become an ugly voice in their life) or they will wisely remove themselves from my presence.

So how do we shut down that ugly voice that can turn what we love to do into a pity party?

Here is a list of six "ordinary" truths that can make your holiday preparations "extraordinary." Let's step out of our circle of expectation (I have to do all this stuff to make sure everyone has a great Christmas), and get a different perspective. Ready?

1. Make a list of what you REALLY want to accomplish, and scratch off the one you like the least. You'll discover that Christmas still happens. It's okay not to send Christmas cards if you do not enjoy the process.

2. Your idea of a "perfect" Christmas is not necessarily everyone else's. People enjoy comfort above perfection.

3. Trying to impress others is really only self-adoration. Think about it. Ouch. Are others blessed by your efforts, or intimidated and shamed?

4. Create out of love, not out of obligation. Obligation isn't nearly as beautiful.

5. Starbuck's is not the true source of your strength and power. Stay in God's Word this holidayseason and you will find the encouragement

that not only you need, but that you can share with others.

"The Lord gives strength to those who are weary. Even young people get tired, then stumble and fall. But those who trust the Lord will find new strength. They will be strong like eagles soaring upward on wings; they will walk and run without getting tired"(Isaiah 40:29-31 CEVUS06). (Take that to the mall with you!!!)

6. Thank God for your creative abilities. Use them not only to serve others, but also to bless HIM: "Your faith in the Lord and your service are like a sacrifice offered to him" (Philippians 2:17 CEVUS06).

After all, Christmas is actually His party, not yours.

May your Christmas season be a sincere celebration of the birth of our Savior - have fun!

1 2 3 4 5 6 7 8 9 10

2 ~ TEN TIPS FOR KEEPING CHRIST IN A FAMILY CHRISTMAS

JANE LANDRETH

As Christmas draws near, families are busy shopping, decorating, baking, and tackling many other tasks that develop during this time of the year. But in the bustle and hurry to get things done, sometimes we forget the real reason for Christmas—Jesus' birth.

Just how can families recapture Christ—keep Christ in the Christmas season? It is up to each family to decide they really want a Christ-filled Christmas. Once that commitment is made, the steps for such a Christmas will fall into place. Here are ten steps to help families keep Christ in Christmas:

1. Get Ready Early--Preparation for Christmas often centers around early shopping, baking, and decorating the tree. A family that takes time to prepare their hearts first will find the true meaning of Christmas. During Advent, time can be set aside, weekly or daily, to worship together. Worship with Bible study, prayer and a discussion of the spiritual meaning of Christmas. Preparation of an Advent wreath can be a family project, with the family talking about the meaning of each candle. Talk about gift-giving. Remind the children that they are gifts from God. Tell the children that the greatest gift is from God, the gift of His Son who was born in a manger. That is the reason for celebrating Christmas.

2. Nativity Scene--A crèche or nativity scene occupying a special place in the home can be meaningful in relating the birth of Jesus to Christmas. Set up the nativity scene preceding Christmas. The setting up of the scene can be spread over the weeks. Set Mary, Joseph and Baby Jesus up first and let the children recall who they are and their part in the Christmas story. Later add shepherds. Remember that the wise men came to the house when Jesus was a young child. A nativity scene outdoors with life-size figures could be a family project. The scene might help others as they pass by to remember the true meaning of Christmas.

3. Christmas Caroling--Christmas is a time for joy and praise. Why not share some of that joy and praise with others by going caroling as a family? If your family is small, you may want to go with other families or a church group. Many groups carol at nursing homes. You may want to carol in a shut-in's home or in the neighborhood. Select some areas and homes to visit ahead of time. Check with them to see if it is appropriate for your family to come caroling. At the close of the caroling, return home for hot chocolate and cookies. You may want to continue caroling as a family in the home.

4. Birthday Cake for Jesus--Birthday cakes are something that even small children can understand. Having one at Christmastime helps the children comprehend the real reason for celebrating Christmas. It is Jesus' birthday. See if you can make the celebration of Jesus's birthday a happy time in your home. Place candles on the "Jesus birthday cake." Sing and blow out the candles.

5. Remembering Those Special Helpers--Christmastime is traditionally a time when families are together and gifts are exchanged. It can become a time of teaching children to think of others. Ask the children who their special helpers are. They could be teachers, bus drivers, doctors, policemen, or just friends. Let the children help prepare a small gift of appreciation for those people. They may want to make cookies or candy and wrap them for their special helpers. A note of appreciation or a card signed by each family member can express gratitude to that special person.

6. Contribute to the Needy--Many communities have a drive to collect clothing, food, and toys at Christmastime to give to the needy. Lead your family in selecting a worthwhile cause or needy person to receive gifts from all of you. Teach the children that God met the world's greatest need by sending His Son, Jesus. We can help meet needs through our gifts of love.

7. "Adopt" Someone -- Is there a nursing home, hospital, or children's home near you? Christmas can be a lonely and unhappy time for people in institutions. Your family may want to adopt a child or senior adult, sending him or her a Christmas gift and visiting him or her at the holiday season. It might even be possible for that person to visit in your home at this time.

8. Share Your Christmas Meal--In the same spirit, your family may want to share a meal with an elderly person or someone who lives alone or with someone who will not be with their family at Christmas. The invitation may include an invitation to share in some of the preparations of Christmas, such as trimming the tree or baking cookies.

9. Family Gifts of Service--Presents under the tree are one of the happy ways to celebrate Christmas, but sometimes there is too much emphasis on material things. Doing things for one another can be far more priceless than any gift purchased. These gifts can be written on a piece of paper, tucked in a box, and gift-wrapped. Each gift should be unique. It is fun to think up the gifts. A father's gift might be a promise to teach a child how to build a birdhouse or take a child to a ball game. Mom's gift to Dad might be to make his favorite dessert. A child may give Mother a gift of setting the table for dinner. Get the idea? Try making your own gifts.

10. Family Worship--Nothing emphasizes the true meaning of Christmas more than worshiping together as a family. Many churches have a worship time on Christmas Eve or early Christmas morning. Many families hold their own Christmas worship around the Christmas tree on Christmas Eve or Christmas morning. It is a meaningful time when the Christmas story is read from the Bible and carols are sung. The family joins together in prayer, thanking God for His Son, Jesus. Whether you decide to celebrate Christmas at church or at home, include time to worship the Christ Child during your Christmas season.

Perhaps you have other ways to keep Christ in Christmas as you teach your children that Christmas is more than gifts, lights and glitter, programs and decorations. Christmas is the birthday of our Lord! Let's first celebrate our Savior with joy, love, and praise, together as a family and let that joy and love flow to others, not only at Christmas time, but also all through the year.

3 ~ AND JESUS SMILED

DIANNE COX

Thanksgiving is over - now we prepare for Christmas!

The children have their own small Nativity that is placed on a TV tray standing in the corner of our family room. After setting up the tray, we cover it with a glistening snow drape. The wood stable is carefully unwrapped and placed on top of the "snow." There are giggles and ahs and gleeful sounds as they unwrap the remaining pieces. The angel and star are carefully placed on top of the stable. They put the big animals inside the stable so they can keep Baby Jesus warm when He arrives. Outside they position the shepherds and their sheep.

Next, they prepare their gift for Jesus. The children help gather foam cups, potting soil and Christmas grass seeds. Each child has his or his own cup to care for. They water and watch for the first sign of fuzzy grass growing. The cups are stored on the kitchen counter and they watch and water daily. A favorite pastime while waiting for the grass to get tall and thick, is playing with the animals and shepherds in and around the stable. December is full of the usual hustle and bustle of activity - decorating, shopping, wrapping, card writing, baking, reading Christmas books and listening to Christmas carols, as well as *Here Comes Santa Claus.*

At last! It is the day before Christmas - time to prepare their gift for the about-to-be-born Babe. They carefully cut the grass in small amounts, about two inches long, and place it on wax paper. While the grass is drying, we make and frost cupcakes. The long awaited Christmas Eve has arrived and the children are full of excitement! After bath time, we read the Christmas story in Luke 2:1-20. Then Mary and Joseph are put in the stable. We also read "The Night Before Christmas" and put out cookies and milk for Santa.

Christmas Day has arrived and it is time for the children to complete their Nativity. We gather in the kitchen to prepare for the grand march. One child carries Baby Jesus, one has the grass, another the Three Wise Men and the last carries a cupcake with a lit birthday candle. As our procession goes from the kitchen to the family room, we all sing "Happy Birthday" to Jesus. The grass turned straw is laid down to make a soft bed for Baby Jesus Who is placed between Mary and Joseph. The Three Wise Men are put outside the stable with their gifts for Jesus. Then we all eat cupcakes!

And Jesus smiled!

4 ~ WE LIVED IN A BARN ONE CHRISTMAS

MARY DEMUTH

The Christmas of 2006 we were homeless. We didn't have keys. Not to a car, not to a home. We'd flown halfway around the world, leaving behind a ministry we toiled over. **Much, particularly in our hearts, lay in ruins.**

Some friends owned **Sabine Creek Ranch,** and on their grounds stood a barn. A tiny apartment was tucked inside a horse and cow barn, flanked by a red caboose and hundreds of acres of Texas pasturelands. We'd never been there before, so we followed directions at night, **making plenty of wrong turns.**

When we found the place, we drove a borrowed car over the cattle guard toward **what would be our home for a month**.

String lights illuminated a small porch, a window and a door in the corner of an aluminum-sided barn. We hefted large pieces of luggage to the apartment. I cannot tell you how bone-tired I was. I hoped to drop my bags, crawl into bed, and cry myself to sleep.

But when we opened the door, Love welcomed us.

The place, usually completely unfurnished in the winter, had been decked out with just the right amount of beds, couches, and tables. The pantry burst at the seams. We had dishes and garbage cans, and cups and forks and food. **But even more, we had a Christmas tree.**

Friends had hijacked the place, decorating it for Christmas. **Cookies preened on the table.**

I will never, ever forget that Christmas. We had so little. Even our relationships with each other felt raw and frayed. We felt the painful burden of failure after leaving France's shores as "going home" missionaries. **But we were loved, so terribly and wonderfully loved.**

Christmas felt right there, in a barn. We heard the nickering of horses, the meowing of kittens, the clop of hooves against the barn floor. Chickens and goats and cows served as a holy object lesson of the incarnation.

Although we were warm and clothed, we understood more keenly the Savior's homelessness, how He left the splendor of heaven for the sodden earth. **We experienced barnyard life alongside Him, without much to call our own except our Heavenly Father and our tired, yet sweet family.**

Jesus was enough, that Christmas. **And He will always be enough.**

5 ~ THE MANGER SCENE THROUGH THE EYES OF A CHILD

ROSAMARY GILLIGAN

As grown-ups, we often look upon the manger scene and see just that, a stable or cave. In it are figurines of Joseph, Mary, Jesus, shepherds, wise men, maybe an angel, and almost always some barnyard animals. Too often, I fear that all we see are little pieces of ceramic, plastic, wood or glass. This past year I was delighted when my manger scene "came to life" – through the eyes of a two-year-old child.

We shall begin with Joseph, the father, or daddy as we say in our area. "The baby has a daddy!" my little one cries in jubilation! Yet a note of respectfulness is present also, in the tone of her voice and character, as the "daddy" interacts with the little Jesus. "Daddy!" That person who fills our home with his presence, but with whom we are a little shy at times. This is likely because he spends much of his time away from our presence providing for our needs. Yet this we know, when he holds us in his lap, and wraps his arms of love around us, we give him all our heart and devotion. Even at age two.

Next we have Mary, the mother. She sits, or kneels in most scenes, so silent and quiet. Not to this little girl. Mamma almost never sits in one place. She is everywhere! She is fixing food, cleaning the house, reading her Bible, and most importantly, she is taking care of her children. She especially gives the baby much attention, to whom all little hearts are drawn. How the little ones love their own mothers, so naturally the mother in the stable is special too.

And then the "fun" characters. There, quietly on the hill or in the greenery, sit the shepherds and their sheep. But alas! This must not be! Sheep are lively and fun. They run and jump. And shepherds must take care of them. One gets caught in a thicket, but it's okay, because the shepherd will set it free. Another falls down, but again, its protector picks it up. What a foundation is being laid, in the little mind, until the day she learns of the "Good Shepherd" and His care for her, as His little lamb.

Unlike the shepherds, even a little one senses the slower more serious nature of the wise men. The children are intrigued with the camels, for who has a camel in their barn? Also, the dark, royal colors of their robes are noticed and exclaimed over. Most importantly, they each carry a gift! Well, a gift is a little formal for this small one. "They have presents!" she cries out. "Presents for baby Jesus!" They are fascinated by the big words, like *frankincense* and *myrrh*. How sad their little hearts would be if they knew the significance of the gifts being given. For today, they are just happy that the wise men have come to see Jesus.

From here we go to the angel, or angels, depending on your setup. "Glory to God in the highest! Peace, goodwill toward men!" Some will argue whether the words were spoken or sung, but to a child everything is put to music. How they love to sing with the angels, "Glory to God! Jesus is born!" Over and over rings the sound, until it can surely be heard in the hills surrounding us. Imagine the thought of all those angels! Suddenly the heavens were "filled" with angels. We adults see a few angels. Ten, twenty, maybe even a hundred. But not a child! She sees a sky with angels outnumbering the stars! There is not even standing room on the stage in their minds! Oh, to see it through their eyes!

Baby Jesus! By far the most important character in this scene! You have not only a baby—the delight of most little ones, but "He is GOD," they whisper. How do their little hearts know to love Him so? Just the mention of His name is special to them. Maybe it's because they see Him first as a little one like them. Perhaps it's because they have heard their parents and grandparents give praise to His name.

Some are troubled that we would worship Jesus as a baby, but not me. He was GOD, GOD from the very beginning! The Bible tells us that He knew no sin. What a role model for little people, and big ones too! Maybe they just feel His love, for we know He said, "Let the little ones come to Me," (Matthew 19:14 RSV) and "Unless you become as a little one, you shall not enter My kingdom" (Matthew 18:3 RSV).

This we know: the little ones love Baby Jesus in the manger; He is often missing when we set up the scene each year! This last year our granddaughter kept the little Jesus figurine on her changing table the whole year. She would get quite upset when anyone would take *her* "Baby Jesus!" He had been carried around with her and placed close to where she could see Him always. We look forward to the day when she learns she can have Jesus with her, at all times, when she puts her trust in His death, burial and resurrection, for her sins. How complete will be her joy to know she can have Jesus always and forever!

Finally, all of our characters have been rearranged. The shepherds and sheep have left their pastures. The wise men and camels have gathered closer. Joseph and Mary, too, have left their stiff kneeling positions and are now bowed over, worshipping Jesus. How does the little one know it says, "They came and fell down and worshipped Him"? (Matthew 2:11 RSV) Yet this part of the reenactment is never left out. How precious to hear them say, "We worship you, Jesus."

How do I know this is what they see? How do I know this is what they feel? I know because I, too, was this little girl many years ago. My prayer today is, "May I never, never, quite grow up, so that I, too, may fully picture what the little ones see when they look into the manger scene." I, too, want to worship Jesus.

"Be near me, Lord Jesus
I ask You to stay,
Close by me forever
And love me I pray.
Bless all the dear children
In Thy tender care,
And fit us for heaven
To live with Thee there."

(To see and hear more lyrics from the public domain hymn entitled "Away in a Manger," readers are invited to find them on YouTube. In the following version, children sing the lyrics: https://www.youtube.com/watch?v=M2ULTkNmIEY)

6 ~ CHRISTMAS IN A CASTLE

ANNA LISA ALVARADO

*II Corinthians 8:9 says, "...the grace of our Lord Jesus
Christ,...though He was rich, yet for your sakes He became poor that we
through His poverty might be rich."*

My husband passed by his own hand in May of '07. The nightmare of
devastation that was left for me to deal with in the wake of his death
weighed upon me like a nuclear war's mushroom cloud of darkness
overhead. I woke every morning with fresh and deepening desperation as
I struggled to maintain some semblance of normalcy in my work and my
life in general.

In a flash, a very unproductive and desolate year had passed. Then, news
came from corporate headquarters. From one minute to the next I knew I
could no longer work for the company for ethical reasons. To stay true to
my own personal standards I knew I had to walk away from my job. My
career and the money that went with it were gone. This realization hit
hard. Watching my funds dwindle, I fervently cried out to the Lord for
yet another year.

Strangely, I felt led of God to only wait on Him and not look for other
work. "...in quietness and confidence shall be your strength..." (Isaiah

30:15). So, I waited. And God waited. "And therefore will the LORD wait, that He may be gracious unto you," (Isaiah 30:18a). Oh how I hate waiting! But I find only when I am desperate do I truly seek the LORD with my whole heart. "And ye shall seek Me, and find Me, when ye shall search for Me with your whole heart" (Jeremiah 29:13).

Out of the blue, in June I was offered a wonderful job. As I was poised to sign on the dotted line, I was torn between God's admonition to rest and wait in quiet confidence and feeling irresponsible if I did not accept a perfectly good job offer. Then it was pointed out that I would not be able to break the contract or leave the area for two years and to "please sign here." I laid the pen down and heard myself say I could not take the job. The sensation of throwing myself off a cliff immediately followed. I went home to contact the local food bank for their hours and location and to continue researching how one can survive on the street. "But fear not thou, O My servant…and be not dismayed…for, behold, I will save thee from afar off" (Jeremiah 46:27a).

Within a week a call came from "afar off."

The familiar voice on the other end was aggravatingly perky. Such brazen happiness was almost an affront to my broken heart and wounded soul. Surely I could not have heard what I thought I heard. It seemed like she asked me something whether I'd be willing to accept an invitation to "come live in a castle and enjoy a European vacation."

My sister and brother-in-law had been transferred from Italy to Belgium and were getting settled into a castle ("château" in French). There was plenty of room and they thought I might enjoy new scenery and some time away. When finally I came to myself and found my tongue, I answered, "Why, yes. I think I would." I got off the phone and, feeling like I had just been thrown a lifeline, decided that in the battle of faith versus sight, free-falling off a cliff isn't so bad when you experience "The eternal God is [your] refuge, and underneath are the everlasting arms" (Deuteronomy 33:27).

I soon found myself on a Boeing 777 on my way to Brussels. Still experiencing numbness from the struggles of the past months, I had to make a conscious effort to be in the moment. The morning dawned in shades of pink and purple and I was enjoying my continental breakfast while we flew over the Celtic Sea. At last I landed in Belgium and was gathered into the warm embrace of my sweet and smiling family.

Having not slept much on the flight, I arrived sleepy and tired which was quickly overcome by excitement of being whisked off to lunch at a sidewalk café. How grateful I was for the walk down old cobblestone streets, beholding the art of ancient architecture, sampling fine chocolates, for a sister who bought some for me, a nephew to get to know again, and a brother-in-law who cared and wasn't afraid to show it. There was the fun of fighting jet lag with fabulously strong Belgian coffee and world-class pastries in the afternoon at yet another picture-perfect sidewalk café. But the best was yet to come.

From Brussels, we traveled about an hour and a half south to a lovely village called Rouveroy, just one mile from the French border. Here we turned into a drive that led to a huge beautiful gate. Past the gate was an ancient bridge that carried us over a picturesque moat. Looking up, I beheld the castle that would become my home while in Belgium. "Eye hath not seen, nor ear heard, neither hath entered the heart of man, the things which God hath prepared for them that love Him" (I Corinthians 2:9).

Over the next few weeks I got to visit Bruges, Mons, Antwerp, and Ghent just to name a few of my favorite places in Belgium. We also traveled to Paris, only two hours away. I saw the Alps of Bavaria and so much more. On lazier days we would stroll over the moat, past the gate, and enjoy the sweet wild plums as we walked the mile southward to France taking in the beautiful fields of poppies.

In Belgium, the law is such that you are welcome to visit for the first 90 days. However, on that 91st day, you either need to be working or on your way out. So, two months into my European vacation, I was invited to stay longer if I—by some miracle—could find work.

And so I did!

Work was fascinating; I got to connect with people of many tongues and nations. The 45 minute commute to and from work was scenic and full of expectation. Though my job hindered some of the travel and sightseeing, it didn't end it completely. I still got to enjoy happy and memorable day trips, but now with a little money in my pocket.

My sister is ever selflessly employing her gifts, "like the merchants' ships [brought] her food from afar" (Proverbs 31:14). Often I would approach the castle in the evening to find flickering candlelight in the windows. Exiting the car, my senses enjoyed the aroma of delicacies and the caress of music transporting me to the land from whence those delicacies had come. It all spoke love to my broken heart lavished upon me from the hand of God like a healing balm…but the best was yet to come.

October had come and was almost past. Looking out the big windows of the château, I relished the sight of the trees lining the moat, sporting their bright fall colors. Like golden weightless coins, the leaves fluttered and fell in the sunshine.

Then November came storming in with cold sheets of slanted rain blowing past and against the windows. This served only to magnify the warmth, love, and security I felt within the castle walls. Through all this, as constant a companion as my own heartbeat, were my thoughts and prayers for my children and their families whom I missed so very much. Were they ok? What were they doing?

I supposed my daughter, son-in-law, and grandson in Houston, Texas, were busy with the duties of young family life. In a foreign and desolate land, my son willingly faced the enemy on the frontlines to protect the country from which he was so very far away. My daughter-in-law's heart was with him in the field of that foreign land. When would I see any of them again?

"Grafenwöhr Unit to Hold Daylong Welcome Home," read the title in the newspaper. My son would be returning to his home base in Germany just in time for Christmas! Germany wasn't too far from Belgium. They would be so happy to make the trip to the castle. My daughter and her family were always up for some travel and more than willing to make the overseas journey for a real family reunion. I could hardly wait!

My heart has forever captured that morning of Christmas in a castle, with snow dazzling in the sunlight, when we gathered to celebrate the lowly birth of our Lord Jesus, the Savior of the world. It was as if we had been dropped into the middle of a movie set, but even better, because God had directed it all. The selflessness of both my brother-in-law's generosity and my sister's handiwork treated our senses to sumptuous aromas, tastes, sights, and sounds. I found myself asking the Lord to give me the grace to handle all the goodness He had lavished upon me.

Today as I meditate upon the amazing gifts God granted this poor widow that Christmas, I know we can have hope for our future because Jesus now sits as "our High Priest of good things to come" for all who put their trust in Him (Hebrews 9:11a).

Editor's note: KJV version of the Holy Bible was used throughout Anna Lisa Alvarado's submission.

7 ~ CHRISTMAS IN A PRISON
THE MESSAGE OF THE BELLS

HARALAN POPOV

(Excerpts from <u>Tortured for His Faith,</u> "Door of Hope" Magazine, December 1986, and Door of Hope International December mailing, (year undetermined). Reprinted by permission of Door of Hope International)

It was December 1952. I was a prisoner of the Communists in Bulgaria, my homeland. I was sent with a hundred other prisoners, to a small island to save some construction material from water damage… The Danube River was expected to flood. Day after day, the river swelled up and up. This day the river flooded the island on which we worked.

The island was divided into two sections. On the opposite side was the concentration camp for 150 women. The men were in charge of raising pigs.

I was ordered to find a raft…and bring some material to the shore where the women and other prisoners were. The material was loaded, and I started to sail. I was in the middle of the flooded river, when suddenly the raft simply came apart beneath me and I was deposited in the freezing water. I was a half-mile from shore, caught up in the swollen, raging river ... wearing a heavy coat and boots... and so frozen, I couldn't move. I was dragged downstream by the current and went under several times, but somehow managed to come back up. I was frozen through by the icy water, the boots dragged me down, the swift current pulled me along.

There was no human way out of this. Death was as certain as it could be.... My whole body was numb from the icy water. The swift current, the heavy boots and coat were dragging me under again and again. Still I fought back to the surface, only to go under again. My strength was completely gone. I gave up struggling...

With a final breath I cried out, "Lord, help me!"... I felt the invisible hands of the Lord supporting me.... Incredibly, I was able to pull myself along...It was truly God's strength, for I had none left. I said over and over, "Thank You, Lord."...I finally reached the shore and saw something which I will never forget.

There had been a trial against the Catholic Church, like the trial against me and the other pastors four years before. Many priests and nuns were sentenced; some were very young. From this trial, there were two nuns in the women's camp.

Everything on the island was covered with mud because of the flood. When we tried to lift one leg to walk, the other leg would sink into the mud up to the knee.

There were some women carrying bundles walking along the shore. A policewoman was guarding them with a rifle in her hand. One of the nuns tried to lift her leg and could not. She threw down her bundle and said to the guard, "I cannot walk." The guard walked over to the nun and kicked her. ...The nun fell on her face into the mud.

I had just gotten out of the water and witnessed this brutality. Never was I so bitter in my heart. I cried out in despair, "Oh God, why am I here?

Why is this nun lying helplessly in the mud? Why do You allow such inhumane treatment? …"

Two miles away there was a large Catholic church. Its bells started to ring, announcing Christmas Eve. It is difficult, of course, for prisoners to keep track of time. But when the bells started to ring, I realized that it was Christmas Eve.

It was like a sermon preached to me. It wasn't just the sound of the bells; words were spoken to my heart: "This day Christ was born. For this new-born Savior, there have been many victims and martyrs. For the same new-born Savior, this nun lies in the mud and you are here."

I'll never forget that Christmas. I was lying exhausted and the two nuns were sinking deeper into the mud. We stopped our struggling and listened. It was dark and freezing cold. I was almost a solid block of ice. The bells could be heard faintly far off in the distance ringing out the message of the Savior's birth.

Tears rolled down my cheeks as I lay there. They were tears of joy because I had not drowned and tears of sorrow because neither the nuns nor I were here for any crimes we had committed. We were here for His sake--- He who was born in a stable on that night so long ago.

I thought of the martyrs of the past: …mothers whose children Herod had killed; the saints who were stoned to death; the thousands burned to death, bound to stakes; the thousands thrown to lions. Church history is stained with the blood of thousands of Christian martyrs because they had received God's Son for whom those bells now tolled. These martyrs were not blind fanatics, but men and women with a faith that lasted unto death. The faith that overcomes death has no fear. Instead there is joy and a song!

I relived the past as the bells rang. I looked at the nuns. Tears were coursing down their cheeks as well.

We wept. We said not a word, but we understood each other.

When the bells stopped, the present reality came rushing back, but the

Voice of God spoke to my heart, "This they have done to My children through the ages, and this they do to you for My sake."

Pastor Haralan Popov pastored the largest Protestant church in Bulgaria. Because of the Communist occupation of Bulgaria, Pastor Popov spent thirteen years and two months in sixteen different prisons and slave camps. Upon his release, he created a ministry to the Persecuted Church known as Evangelism to Communist Lands, now known as Door of Hope International, located in Glendale, California. Pastor Popov died November 14, 1988. The ministry continues under the direction of his son, Paul Popov.

8 ~ SWEDISH CHRISTMAS EVE

MARILYN SEYMOUR

As a little girl, I remember our Christmas Eve gathering as the event to prove Christmas was really upon us. The anticipation had finally brought us to the point of action and the celebration would now begin.

With the short cold days and the early starlit night, we would gather the boxes of presents and Mom's special food contributions to drive to our Swedish Grandpa and Grandma's.

The steamed window of the front door that led into the bustling kitchen would be our welcome. Upon entering, the aroma of the awaiting feast would bombard the previous pristine fresh air we had experienced on our drive.

The children had the sacred responsibility of placing the presents under the aluminum tree upon which hung shiny blue balls. The excitement of seeing one's name on a present reminded each child that they were remembered and were special. I remember thinking good gifts came in big packages, a concept that would be challenged every year until I finally realized it was untrue.

The women were busy completing the meal preparations; it had to be just right when the grace was prayed. My grandmother was confined to a homemade, wooden stool with wheels on the legs to get around. She would oversee the Swedish meatballs, poking and turning them in a large round skillet. To see them, one might think they were burnt, but, no, they were browned to perfection with the juicy flavor only Grandma could attain.

We also served lutefisk in white sauce which I can now admit I never tasted, and ham. We carried pickled herring, pickled beets, Swedish brown beans, and both a red and a green Jell-O salad to the long oval oak table. The potatoes were especially good because they were squeezed through the ricer colander into a glass bowl decorated with painted flowers. Those potatoes were light and fluffy but could soak the delicious gravy as no other type of potatoes could. We, of course, also had homemade bread, thanks to my mom. As far as dessert, it was the creation of Aunt Alice and Mom that always amazed our "sweet tooth."

The children encouraged the adults to eat quickly, because the meal had to be completed and the dishes washed before presents could be passed. I remember the ladies warming the dish water on the cast iron stove and pouring it into the oval white enamel dish pan with a few drops of Joy to get those dishes clean. I think I usually helped dry the dishes because the water was too hot for little hands. The women seemed to be so joyous on this occasion, probably realizing the cooperative success of such a feast for their families.

Then we would all gather around the tree and the children would start handing out the presents. I remember there were a lot of socks and gloves or handkerchiefs for the men. The ladies received gloves, stationery, hand lotion, and candy. We kids each had our "Oohs" and "Ahhs." Who wouldn't be happy with jewelry or "Evening in Paris" perfume?

The Swedish Christmas Eve was a wonderful tradition that I have had to adjust a little for my family, but the foundation continues to be observed even down to the Swedish meatballs and Swedish brown beans.

Editor's Note: Swedish Brown Beans? Find them and other Swedish foods at Marilyn's Christmas Eve celebrations in the Recipe section.

9 ~ A TEXT FROM HEAVEN

MARILYN BOONE

Heaven and earth are only three feet apart, but in the thin places
that distance is even shorter. ~ A Celtic Saying

It was almost midnight that Christmas Eve, and my heart was heavy. My mother had passed away only two weeks earlier, and I missed her terribly. Christmas had always been my favorite holiday, but there was hardly a moment when I wasn't wishing I could have given her one more hug or told her I loved her one more time.

While the rest of the family had already gone to bed, I was still awake, working in the kitchen. Alone with my thoughts, I was struggling to finish preparing the food we would eat the next morning after opening gifts. The sausage egg casserole and the monkey bread were traditions I didn't want to break, but grief had dampened my spirits and numbed my senses. Like every other task I had faced since my mother's funeral, simply going through the motions was an effort. I decided to step outside in hopes that a breath of cold, fresh air might somehow make me feel better.

The night that greeted me was one of intense quiet, as if a hush had settled over the earth. I remembered what I had read about the Celtic belief in thin places, locations where the veil between this world and the divine is unusually thin. It was in nearby fields on that very first Christmas night when the veil was lifted and first an angel, and then a multitude of angels, appeared before the shepherds watching their flock and proclaimed the birth of Jesus. While I wasn't a shepherd in a field of sheep, it was Christmas, and I imagined the possibility that in the silence, in the middle of my driveway, I might be standing in a thin place.

*Silent night, holy night…*the words began singing in my head as my eyes gazed into the starlit sky spread above me.

*All is calm, all is bright…*the song continued. Tears blurred the sight while I whispered heavenward, "Merry Christmas, Mom."

*Sleep in heavenly peace…*brought the song to an end. Reluctantly, I took one more deep breath and headed back into the house. Sleep had been elusive and was something I needed. With Christmas morning a short time away, I vowed to try to get in at least a few hours.

On my way back through the kitchen, I picked up my cell phone to take with me and came to an immediate stop. It showed I had received a new text message while I was outside. There was no name, only the sender's phone number. I swiped my finger across the screen to read it.

"Merry Christmas, Marilyn," was all the text said.

Staring at the screen, I felt my heart beating as if it were racing to come to life again. Had the words just said, "Merry Christmas," I would have figured it was part of a group message from someone. But this one included my name. This one was personal.

I started comparing the number with others in my contact list, curious to find out who sent it. After several minutes of looking, however, the identity of the sender remained a mystery. My mind continued to scour every possibility, both earthly and divine, until I couldn't help but smile. *Could there indeed be a heavenly cell phone?*

Though a part of me wasn't sure it wanted an answer, I sat down at the table and kept searching. It didn't take much longer to discover the text was sent by an old friend from elementary school. A business card I found confirmed the phone number. Our paths had crossed unexpectedly a few years earlier, though I hadn't seen or heard from him since. The mystery of who sent it had been solved, but I still found myself in a state of wonderment. He wouldn't have known about my mother, or the message I had spoken outside, yet the timing of his text couldn't have been more perfect.

Some might call this coming together of circumstances a coincidence, but I prefer to think of it as one of those moments God uses to touch us in unique and unexpected ways. God's timing is always perfect, and only He knew how much I needed to receive that text at the exact time I did. Through a heavenly nudge to an old friend, the joy found in the real reason for the season was renewed within me, despite my heartache. I know that's what my mother would have hoped for.

Don't ever hesitate to say, "Merry Christmas," for you never know whose life you may bless.

Editor's Note: Marilyn Boone mentioned she needed to prepare their traditional Christmas morning breakfast ... and those Christmas morning recipes are included in the "Recipe" section. They might become a favorite for your family as well.

10 ~ BRANTFORD COVENANT CHURCH
A SPECIAL BLESSING
TO THE COMMUNITY

JIM KISBY

I have always looked forward to Christmas. When I first began going to school in the fall, I would be counting down the days until Christmas. You are probably saying that was because I was looking forward to being out of school for a couple of weeks. That might have had a little to do with it, but there was a bigger and more compelling reason. I believe my countdown toward Christmas was because the Bible verses telling about the birth of Christ and how the angels announced his birth are something that strikes a note of awe in the heart of everyone who hears them.

At least during the 1940s and 1950s, the Children's Christmas Program at the Brantford Evangelical Covenant Church in north-central Kansas was held on Dec. 25th - Christmas night. That evening program drew the largest crowds of any church service during the year. The ushers always had to put extra chairs up and down the aisle and sometimes in the foyer in the back to accommodate people of the community who wanted to hear the children present that wonderful story about Jesus in songs, in dialog, and in reciting memorized verses.

A few weeks before Christmas, Sunday School teachers had given children Bible verses or "pieces" that usually rhymed so the children would retell the Biblical Christmas story. Probably most kids rehearsed their "piece" a few times even on Christmas Day. Kids and parents, and grandparents, all wanted the program to run smoothly and to be ready when it was the child's turn to help the audience hear:

> *"And it came to pass in those days, that there went out a decree from Caesar Augustus... And all went to be taxed... And Joseph also went up from Galilee... unto the city of David, which is called Bethlehem... to be taxed with Mary his espoused wife, being great with child. And so it was, that, while they were there... she brought forth her firstborn son, and wrapped him in swaddling clothes, and laid him in a manger; because there was no room for them in the inn...Shepherds....angels, 'Fear not...unto you is born this day...a Savior, which is Christ the Lord...Glory to God in the highest, and on earth peace, good will toward men'" (from Luke 2, K JV).*

The youngest children often sang "Away in a Manger" as they rocked their imaginary Baby Jesus, used their hands to lay down their sweet heads, and spread their chubby little fingers above them to twinkle the "stars" looking down on the wonder of God's Son coming to sleep in a manger on that first Christmas night.

Other classes did their recitations and sang their special music selections, but we were all stirred at the sound of a whole community packed within the church's walls and singing about the Lord Jesus together. Because the Brantford church had begun with a cluster of Swedes, a Christmas service wasn't complete without every Swede singing their song about the Christmas angels. The event was a wonderful opportunity for the Gospel message to be presented to people who may have only come for that one service during the entire year. People seemed to like hanging on to Christmas as long as they could, and many people probably had no place to go on Christmas night because most of the festivities had already come and gone.

I sometimes wonder who all sat in the pews and on those extra chairs on Christmas nights. Some may have been lonely in the quietness that surrounded them at the conclusion of this busy time of the year. Maybe others were thinking about their sons and daughters that were perhaps in the heat of some battle during the time of WWII. A few, perhaps, came because the Holy Spirit put a desire in their hearts to hear this wonderful message about the birth, life, and death of God's Son who came to Bethlehem and offered to be the Savior for any within mankind who would put his or her trust in Him. I don't know the exact reasons the snowy parking areas filled or why so many people scooted close together in the pews of our country church, but there always seemed to be a big interest for many in the surrounding community to be there.

Decades later, Christmas is still one of the highlights of the year for me. Like many young men, in time I moved away for employment, military duty, and married to begin raising a family. The pull, though, for wanting to get home to family and to celebrate Christmas in our country church remained strong. Most years, whether we drove from Colorado, Texas, or Kentucky, we made plans to get back to Kansas for Christmas.

Today my wife and I have family living in more than a couple states and now others keep the farm where I began. Thankfully, though modern farming practices have reduced the number of families living in the area, the same country church is still telling the Christmas story in verses and songs, and knowing that brings me comfort when I think back fondly of these memories from years long ago.

Editor's Note: Jim surprised everyone by winning first place at his Kentucky church's "Men's Cake-Baking Competition." He prepared a favorite Christmas Eve recipe from Christmas Eve's in Kansas. It's called "Deep Dark Secret" and it's included in this book's "Recipe" section. The committee finally told Jim he had to bake something else because his "Deep Dark Secret" cake won year after year.

11 ~ GOD PUT ME ON THE WATER

KEVIN TALTON

From the time I was knee high, my dad took me fishing with him and occasionally took me to work with him on all kinds of vessels before he retired some years ago. I guess it was inevitable that I would end up working on boats. I always wanted to make my dad proud and to follow in his footsteps. But I had no idea how hard work on the water would be until I started professionally in 1993 after high school. Occasionally, I've even had to spend Christmas on the water, especially early in my career.

Maritime life is comprised of long hours in a day. The days become long weeks, and the weeks become long years. In other words, it requires a lot of time away from home. Every position on a boat is hard work starting as a Deckhand, all the way up to the Master (Captain). The captain easily has the most responsibility and stress aboard a boat or ship because he is responsible for the entire vessel, any cargo that may be onboard, and the lives of the crew and passengers. Everything that happens falls on the captain.

Sounds tough doesn't it? Now put into the equation giving your life to Jesus Christ. When we give our lives to God, I believe things get a whole lot harder. Jesus said the road with Him would be difficult -*Matthew 7:13-14.* I believe that part of the difficult road is being despised by the world. Here are some quotes from Jesus Himself...

"If the world hates you, you know that it hated Me before it hated you. If you were of the world, the world would love its own. Yet because you are not of the world, but I chose you out of the world, therefore the world hates you." (John 15:18-19 ESV)

"And you will be hated by all for My name's sake. But he who endures to the end will be saved" (Matthew 10:22 ESV).

The maritime industry is a rough/tough environment. I have worked on fishing boats, dinner cruise boats, passenger ferries, research boats, and tugboats nearly my entire life. I believe there are many more non-believers than followers of Jesus Christ in this line of work. One who loves Christ can feel pretty alone in this field.

Many times since I've been in this field of work I have asked God "Why am I here, and what are You trying to accomplish through me in this time of life?" And quite a few times He has answered me by sending people I wouldn't expect across my path who asked me what I believe and why I believed it. This gives me opportunities to share His good news of the gospel.

I have had other mariners come to me and tell me that I was the reason their language changed for the better, but I know it was the Lord. I have to stay in the Word and am humbled when I'm told by mariners that I've had answers to their questions when others didn't. But I know it was the Lord. I have had a crew member ask me to be their mentor. I know it was the Lord. I could do none of these things without the Lord's help.

Many times that I spend nights on the water whether it be working or a night out on the ocean shark fishing, I look up at the stars and think about a great many things-- like where Heaven is beyond our universe and what my loved ones in Heaven might be doing at that particular moment.

Especially during this time of year, I often find myself thinking about God coming down here to Earth as a baby and what He grew up to do for me, and for all mankind. What evidence of His incredible love for us.

Out on the water, I can reflect on God giving us the stars for signs and seasons. Mariners relied upon the stars for navigation on the oceans and seas until technology began providing us with other means of navigation. Perhaps like me, when you look at the stars this time of year, you can't help but think about the journey of the wise men following the Star of Bethlehem that God had given them to navigate with while obeying the tugging in their hearts to go and seek Him out. Perhaps the next person who asks you or me a question will be someone God guided across a "desert" until they came to hear what you or I have to say about Jesus, the King above all Kings. That's something to think about, isn't it? Will we have spent time with the Lord beforehand so that we'd have a ready answer?

Both the interactions God brings across my path and my own quiet reflections that occur because I'm a mariner are indications of God's answers to my "why am I here" prayers.

Now I continually ask the Lord to send me someone to whom I can talk and encourage for His sake. God's Holy Heaven-sent Son who spent some of His last earthly hours with Peter, a waterman like myself, reminded Peter he was a fisherman turned fisher-of-men.

I believe my Commander has instructed me not only to follow in my earthly father's footsteps, but more importantly, to follow in His.

Editor's Note: Kevin is also an artist and photographer, so keep an eye out for his work or follow him on Facebook.

12 ~ THE TRUE GIFT GIVER, NOT SANTA, CHANGED CEDRIC'S LIFE AND MINE

REPRINTED BY PERMISSION
PENNY ROBICHAUX KOONTZ
AS TOLD TO HARRIETT FORD

"Ah, Christmas time," I think to myself. Leaning back in my favorite wing back chair and looking out my office window at fresh snow on the ground. Lights twinkle on our log home. I see too, lights that wrap around the fence surrounding our yard amid the 70 acres of rolling hills on Jacob's House at Thunder Ranch in Missouri. Remembering Christmases past, I whispered, "Who would have thought things would have turned out like this, Lord?"

The turning point arrived on Christmas of 1991. Little did I know that God would provide in such an amazing way, nor could I have dreamed He would change the course of my entire life.

I had just taken over a homeless shelter, planning to serve God for one year to thank Him that I could walk again after a long struggle to overcome childhood polio which had left me suffering its crippling effects. I thought of those long-ago surgeries, the body cast that started behind my head, circled my neck and encased my body down to my hips for a stretch of two Christmases, concealing what would be my future.

The shelter was a condemned property in a rural area of Texas, pitch-black at night, except for the light from a lonesome train, the midnight special, as it passed by. I had 42 youngsters and 30 adults at the shelter, no money, and the only Christmas ornaments for the tree were those I had collected with my own children over the years.

It was time to decorate and as we were putting the tree up, I noticed the children were grumbling. "Miss Penny, how is Santa ever gonna find us out here in the dark?" I laughed at them and said, "Well, let's sing real loud while we decorate and maybe he'll find his way."

The shelter was so new to the area I didn't expect anyone to find us, not even Santa. A few of the helpers began timidly singing carols. "That's a miserable attempt at joyful singing. I can barely hear you. Let's try Rudolph, and I mean loud! Put your heart into it. Don't you want Santa to hear?"

They upped the volume, and just as we were getting into the song, all voices stopped. A collective intake of breath filled the room. I turned to see what had caused the song to end so quickly and saw the jolly old elf himself, Santa, walking toward me dressed in full red velvet trimmed with snowy white fur. The children's eyes were as big as Frisbees, and you could have heard a snowflake drop.

He whispered to me as he passed by, "Heard you might need a Santa. I'm on my way to a party, and thought I'd stop here first."

Mr. Claus delighted the children, taking them one at a time on his knee and hearing their Christmas wishes. I smiled at their eager eyes and laughter, but to my dismay, each child asked for a new bicycle. After Santa left, the reality hit me. How could I possibly make 42 bikes magically appear on Christmas morning? Silently I prayed, "Lord, how will I ever get that many bikes when just getting enough food for all these people is stretching my faith?"

I certainly knew good Bible verses about how God provides abundantly and exceedingly. But I would never have guessed how specifically God, and *not* Santa, was about to show up.

Soon articles started appearing in the newspaper. Word spread. People brought warm clothes, toiletries, and other items, and yes, the bikes started arriving to be assembled in our secret workshop.

Christmas morning arrived and oh, the bikes...bikes everywhere. Eventually exhausted after all the gift giving, laughter, ribbons, and tears of joy, I decided to head for my room for a needed rest.

As I started out on the dusty path, I heard little feet running behind. "Miss Penny, Miss Penny!" Five-year-old Cedric caught up to me, his cheeks streaked with tears. I knelt on the drive to see what troubled him.

"What is it Cedric? Why are you crying, honey?" I asked.

"I didn't git me no bike! I told Santa I wanted a purple two-wheeler, but Santa didn't git me no bike!"

Dismayed, I groaned inwardly, *how could we have been off by one bike!* Looking into those tear-filled eyes, I said, "Cedric, honey, did you ask Jesus for a bike?"

"No, Miss Penny, I asked Santa."

"Well, that explains it," I said. "You see, Santa Claus is a story about Christmas. He's a one-day wonder. But Jesus is the true Gift and the true gift-giver. He hears you when you pray. So let's talk to Him about this."

Cedric got down on his knees beside me and made quite a noisy plea to Jesus, ending with a request for a purple two-wheeler.

After the "Amen," I looked up to see dust trailing behind a pickup heading along the drive toward us. I was struggling to get up off my knees when the pickup truck screeched to a halt, throwing Texas dust clouds all around us. "Are you Miss Penny?" a man asked, stepping out of his truck.

"That's me," I said, "Can I help you?"

"Sorry I'm late," he said, "I meant to come yesterday, but our children made a surprise visit and I couldn't get away. Can anyone use this?" He lifted a brand new purple bicycle from the pickup's bed and placed it right in front of little Cedric, whose amazed eyes widened with joy.

Woman of great faith that I am, I stood there absolutely speechless and watched God make Himself real to a delighted child. I never got the name of that man who donated that bike.

The joy of that moment is as fresh in my heart today as it was on that morning. And because of that joy, I have continued ministering to homeless adults and children at Jacob's House at Thunder Ranch in Chestnut Ridge, Missouri, helping more than 8,000 individuals and hundreds of youngsters find a future with hope.

I am praying for all who read this story that you also get your purple bike, whatever it may be: **Healing for your body, peace for your mind, and comfort for your heart . . . that only Jesus can bring.**

Editor's Note: To gain more information or to support the ministry mentioned in this article, please email: ***penny@jacobshouse.org***

13 ~ THE BOX

(REPRINTED BY PERMISSION)
ELIZABETH HERMANN STINGLE / BECKY MUELLER

Note from Becky Mueller: *Otto Hermann was my grandfather about whom I had heard stories from others of his generosity throughout my life. Although he died when I was only two, his nature was something I have grown to admire. I believe that memories of "a goodness" that people are remembered by is truly what Christ intended for us. This story was written in 1957 by Otto's sister. In the 1970s, it was found among old history of our family, so my cousin typed it out and framed it as a Christmas gift to the families.*

What made Christmas in my childhood? Certainly not costly gifts, for my family was never in a position, with eight children, to lavish upon us the things the present generation expects and accepts so lightly as their due. No, to us, Christmas was THE BOX!

We lived on a small farm where the land was so poor you couldn't raise a fuss on it, but it did give us a nice out-of-doors setting, and a barn and fields to play in. We learned to know, in the eight years we lived this way, all the trees and plants in the locality. We could not depend upon radio or TV for our recreation, but played and sang together, and often when some particularly interesting book found its way into our possession, we took turns at reading it aloud, thus eliminating the argument as to who had the chance to read it first. Now understand please, I am not advocating a return to the "good old days," which were not always so good, with pot-bellied stoves where one roasted from the front and froze from the rear, and where the only running water to be had was that which you yourself ran for, from the old iron pump. No, indeed. I like my comfort as well as anyone, but one does sometimes wonder if we haven't gone a bit too far in our efforts to raise a standard of living, and something precious was sacrificed in the process.

My sister and I were the youngest members of the family, and our Christmas was just "made" for us by an older brother who operated a little confectioner's store in Uniontown, Kentucky. He loved children, and in particular us, and liked doing nice things for little people. So, when he stocked up his supplies for his Christmas trade, he included a little extra for us. Things we would not otherwise have gotten – the rarer fruits, such as figs and dates, candies, nuts and a few odds and ends, all packed in one of those sturdy old-fashioned wooden cracker boxes, now so seldom seen.

We younger members of the family would begin to ask anxiously as soon as December dawned, "Do you suppose Otto will send THE BOX again this year?" We were not supposed to ask, or even hint, but what a relief it was to our childish minds when we were informed that the sending was on his agenda. Once or twice he did get so busy that the box failed to arrive on the 24th; and once he sent it by river, on one of those boats that use to ply the Ohio, and it got hopelessly lost in the shuffle of more important freight. But for some ten years, it always came, and kept alive for us in our childish hearts a faith in Christmas.

The unpacking of it was a ceremony. Mother was, of course, in general, in charge of the operations and to avoid arguments and dissensions, divided conscientiously piece by piece the contents of THE BOX. There was always a bit of swapping, and more the greedy of us disconsolately licked our chops, when long after our share had disappeared down the hatch, one of the more frugal ones would tantalizingly hold before our eyes a delectable bit he or she could still look forward to eating. We could have wrung each other's neck at times like these.

Even today, the pungent odor of an orange awakens in me a nostalgic memory of that blessed Christmas box, and revives a Christmas spirit sometimes dim. A small thing, maybe, but I wonder if it would not have been a bit better for the world today if Christmas had been kept on a small, simple scale like this.

I wish it were in my power to give someone half the pleasure that was given us, in the receiving of THE BOX.

14 ~ THE CHRISTMAS DOLLS

SYBIL COPELAND

In the year of 1942, families were feeling the effects of World War II. They were struggling to pay their bills and rent, and to even buy groceries. Our father was working as a taxicab driver. Eva, our oldest sister, aged twenty-two, was single, living at home, and working at the General Telephone Company as a switchboard operator. Even though money was tight, everyone seemed to be worrying about presents for Christmas, which was just around the corner.

Sharlene and Shirley, my triplet sisters, and I, aged six, were worried, too. We wondered if there would be many gifts under the Christmas tree for us. When the Sears Roebuck Christmas catalog arrived in our mailbox, we immediately marked our favorite pages. Then, we began dropping hints to our parents. Surely, Santa Claus wouldn't disappoint us this year, as we had been very good little girls.

"I think we should ask for just one gift this Christmas since Dad and Mother are having a hard time feeding and clothing our family," Sharlene remarked to Shirley and me.

"I agree with Sharlene, don't you Sybil?" asked Shirley.

"Yes," I replied nodding in agreement, "so let's decide what we want the most."

After a few minutes of discussion, we decided to ask for new dolls. Could our family afford three? Would we have to share one? Maybe Santa Claus could help our parents by putting three dolls under the Christmas tree this year. If not, we'd be content with getting new coloring books, crayons and reading books.

"Let's ask Mother and Eva to write a letter to Santa Claus for us," Shirley suggested.

"Okay, I think that's a good idea," Sharlene replied. "Don't you, Sybil?"

"Yes, then we can print our names and mail the letter to Santa Claus at the North Pole," I said, smiling at my sisters.

We told Mother and Eva our list to Santa Claus was short this year. In unison we said, "We only want new dolls for Christmas." They helped us write the letter and assured us it would arrive at the North Pole on time.

Early Christmas morning, the smells of fresh coffee and Mother's turkey baking in the oven woke us up. We could hear Bing Crosby singing "White Christmas" on the radio. We bounced out of bed and ran into the kitchen as our family exclaimed, "Merry Christmas girls!" We hopped up and down, hugged everyone and wished them all a Merry Christmas.

"Do we get to open our Christmas presents now?" asked Sharlene, "Or do we have to eat breakfast first?"

"Remember we eat first, then we open our gifts," Mother reminded us.

"Yes, those are the rules, so find your places at the table and we'll eat breakfast," Daddy said.

Once breakfast was over, we rushed into the living room to see what Santa Claus had brought us. The first things we saw were three beautiful dolls under the Christmas tree. We couldn't believe our eyes! We squealed with delight and jumped up and down hugging our new dolls and each other.

Mother asked, "How are you going to tell your dolls apart since they're dressed alike?"

Daddy said, "I'm sure they will figure this out before the day is over, won't you girls?"

"I think we should decide what color nail polish each doll should wear. I want my doll to wear red nail polish," Shirley said.

"I want my doll to wear pink nail polish to match her coat," Sharlene said.

"My doll is going to wear clear nail polish," I said. "Now we can tell them apart since we painted their finger nails a different color."

We spent the rest of Christmas playing with our new gifts. Our dolls were from Santa Claus, but the crayons, coloring books and reading books were from our parents.

Years later, we learned Eva had played Santa Claus that Christmas. She had special ordered our dolls, and paid a little each month on them out of her own salary.

We loved our Christmas dolls, but we loved our sister, Eva, even more!

Today I look back fondly on the memory of the Christmas morning we received those beautiful Christmas dolls and its wonder will always be dear to me.

But, now that many years have passed and I've raised children of my own, I would not leave you readers with just my memories about one Christmas morning for me without telling you this: the greatest gift for all mankind was the birth of Jesus Christ, the true Christmas story, and we taught that truth to our children and grandchildren.

Once I accepted God's gift of salvation, Jesus Christ, I became involved in the Ladies Missions group in my church. It wasn't long before I felt God calling me in a leadership role. God provided many opportunities for my training so I could use my gifts in my church, in our association of several churches, and in my state.

To this day, I feel so blessed to be able to share the good news and I know God isn't through with me yet.

15 ~ WITHOUT PEACE,
CAN THERE BE GOOD WILL?

PAUL WARDER

It was December 20, 1943, just five days before Christmas. Two airplanes were in the sky over Germany. The one was an American B-17, piloted by Lt. Charlie Brown and his crew. The other was a German 109, piloted by Lt. Franz Stigler. Author Adam Makos gives the details in his book "A Higher Call."

In one sense the American bomb crew was looking forward to Christmas; some in their group were hosting a Christmas party for children the next day. One crew member had been hoarding chocolate bars for weeks and wrapping them to be ready to give out as presents. In the early part of the journey, one of the American crew had joked that the flaking frost on the inside of the plane was already making it look like Christmas.

The jovial mood changed when flak guns on the ground and German fighters in the sky engaged the B-17 in combat. These attacks killed one of the American gunners, wounded others, and brought such horrible damage to the plane that the Germans filed a report that the American bomber had been shot down. In fact, it was a miracle that the B-17 was flying at all.

The German pilots, thinking they had scored a kill, flew away. After a while, another German plane approached. This fighter was piloted by Franz Stigler. Stigler got close enough to see the severe damage to the American craft. "How is it still flying?" he wondered.

It would have been extremely easy for Stigler to finish off Charlie Brown's plane, but he had had a "do-unto-others-as-you-would-have–them–do-unto-you" principle drilled into him as part of both his Catholic and his aviation trainings. So, instead, Stigler spent the next ten minutes trying to get the attention of the American crew. First he tried to motion for them to land, which he considered far safer than being shot out of the air. Then he tried communicating on first one side of the plane and then the other, mouthing the word *Sweden* to get Brown's crew to fly the thirty-minute route there rather than the two-hour flight back to England.

As the two planes reached an area heavily manned by German flak guns, the German pilot was still not getting the American craft to respond. So Stigler did the next best thing: he flew in close formation with the B-17 so that the German gunners would not shoot at the Americans' plane for fear of destroying one of their own airplanes.

This whole encounter took only ten minutes, with Franz Stigler finally getting the attention of Charlie Brown long enough to salute him before flying off once he had escorted the American plane past Germany's guns.

The US plane did manage to limp back to England. Both pilots were religious men: Charlie Brown was a man who never missed a Sunday morning worship service and had carried a Bible with him that day; Franz Stigler was a devout Catholic who carried a rosary in his pocket that day as well.

That horrible war brought death and destruction to many who longed for "peace on earth," but for at least ten minutes, five days before Christmas, in the sky, there was one remarkable and courageous instance of "good will toward men."

Both men survived the rest of the war. They were reunited forty-seven years later, in 1990. They remained close friends until, just months apart, both men died in 2008.

Angels heralded Jesus' birth: "Glory to God in the highest, and on earth peace, good will toward men." (Luke 2:14 NKJV)

Over thirty years later Jesus taught His followers: "But I say to you... love your enemies, do good to those who hate you...Treat others the same way you want them to treat you....Be merciful, just as your Father is merciful..." (Luke 6:27, 31, 36 NASB)

16 ~ THAT FIRST CHRISTMAS AWAY FROM HOME

LOREN G. KISBY

The year was 1965. My location was nearly half way around the world in a little country named South Korea. Uncle Sam was my travel agent for my excursion from the heart of the US, Kansas.

At that time, I was Lt. Kisby of Charlie Battery, 5th Battalion, 38th Artillery. We were located north of Munsan-ni. We understood we were the closest artillery unit to North Korea. We were one of a few 105 howitzer batteries that could actually fire a round over the DMZ and into North Korea from our permanent location.

Christmas was nearly upon us. I had about three months of the 13-month deployment behind me. A battalion officers' Christmas party was scheduled for the afternoon and evening. Being the junior officer and a "tea-totaler," the Charlie battery commander asked if I would mind filling the position of "Officer of the Day."

I willingly accepted, which meant I would check on the posted guards on a regular basis and be available if anything out of the normal routine occurred. With that position filled, the rest of the officers climbed into the front and back of a covered ¾ ton military pickup to travel the four or five miles on dirt roads to battalion headquarters for the celebration.

It would have been easy to begin thinking about all of the things taking place 7000 miles away in Kansas. They would certainly be having plum pudding, pickled herring, and of course lutefisk in white sauce over mashed potatoes. In Korea, we would eat well, but none of that would be on the menu. Back home, the Brantford Covenant Church's cantata and children's Christmas program with baby Jesus, Mary and Joseph, and the shepherds were probably already past, but there was still the 11 p.m. gathering with hymns and "Listna" to close out the day. *(In Swedish, the "Listen to the Angels" song title is written "Lyssna på änglarna," but we second-generation Swedes thought we got close enough referring our church's traditional Swedish song as "Listna.")*

When what you are used to is beyond reach, you do what you can. It wasn't dark yet, so I climbed up the hill behind the battery headquarters building. The terrain was almost barren but there were a few small pine trees nearly three feet tall scattered along the hillside. I cut one down and took it back to our barracks, which was a Quonset with a concrete floor.

I don't recall how it was supported, but I set the tree on a small table. We had no decorations but this was still in the day when all bottled beverages required a "church key" to pry off the cap. Gathering a bunch of different colored caps and some string, an ice pick made a nice hole to attach the string to the cap, which was then tied to the branches of the small tree. The tree was decorated!

There was still something missing. Oh, the stockings. Going to each officer's footlocker, I selected a sock. Using a tack, I hung six matching socks along the front of the table, all US Army olive drab.

When the crew arrived back at Charlie battery they were pleasantly surprised. I think that little tree made Christmas away from family a little less difficult.

Oh, I was informed that the little tree I cut down was part of a program to reforest South Korea and was protected from harvesting. Too late.

We all made it through that Christmas with memories to take back home. We also had something for which to be thankful. The Stars and Stripes newspaper was reporting that things were really heating up for our brothers-in-arms in a place called Vietnam. Things weren't so bad in our little part of the world after all.

Have a Merry Christmas,

Loren G. Kisby

17 ~ A SIMPLE CADENCE

NATE LEE

Do you ever struggle with feelings of inadequacy or inferiority? Do you suffer from imposter syndrome where you can't seem to shake the fear that eventually someone is going to peek behind your curtain of confidence to reveal the true wizard of the Emerald City?

For my sake, I hope that your answer is yes because I don't want to be the only one occasionally feeling inferior. I don't know why, but sometimes the holidays can magnify these feelings. Despite the efforts of a particular carol reminding me to have myself a merry little Christmas, I haven't yet had all my troubles rid from my sight.

Many Christmas carols remind us to be merry or joyful. I believe many people, even those who are followers of Christ, whose birthday we celebrate this time of year, find producing merriment-on-demand to be difficult.

Allow me to share a story about a relative of mine that occurred last December. We'll call her Ann. With Christmas fast approaching and much to do, a desperate cry for volunteer help rang throughout Ann's church. Ann, eager to assist in any capacity, raised her hand. "I'll serve," she selflessly replied.

Now, I won't presume to know the motives behind those in charge, but their response was to continue scanning the room around and over Ann's enthusiastic arm waving. "Anyone? Anyone at all. We're not picky. After all, beggars can't be choosers."

There was almost an unspoken message of, "Unless you can come bearing gold, frankincense, and myrrh, don't come at all."

Needless to say, Ann was befuddled and hurt by their rejection. This response to her, "Here I am, send me," did little to extinguish her mounting feelings of inadequacy.

If you have ever had an experience like Ann's, I am truly sorry. Sadly, there will always be those who expect grander levels of pageantry than what we are capable of offering, but that in no way diminishes the value of your offering.

I love music. I like to play the drums. Maybe it's for this reason that the Christmas carol "Little Drummer Boy" has always struck a chord with me. But in light of Ann's story and my own, I've discovered a solace hidden within the lyrics of this carol that runs deeper than the simple "Pa rum pum pum pum."

This young percussionist was poor, just like the newborn Savior whom he had come to worship. He didn't have extravagant gifts to place at the feet of Jesus. No precious metals or costly spices. He did, however, have something that was personally valuable and meaningful which he wanted to share with the King of Kings. A drum. So, perhaps even in spite of the complaints from the inn next door, the little drummer boy offered up what he had. A simple cadence. "Then He smiled at me," the carol ends.

Your offerings of service or praise to God, whether extravagant, simple, or somewhere in the middle, will always bring a proud smile to God's face. He is, after all, the one who gave you your unique gifts.

And speaking of simple, who better than Jesus, the suffering servant, to understand and empathize with us when we're being rejected for being "simple." Jesus had, according to Isaiah 53:2, "...nothing beautiful or majestic about His appearance, nothing to attract us to Him." In fact, most people entirely overlooked Him and His reason for coming. The people of that time were so busy looking for a king who would rescue them from the physical oppression under which they had suffered for so very long that they missed God's only Son who came to release mankind from our spiritual oppression. Their hopes were so set on someone who appeared kingly that they dismissed a simple carpenter from Nazareth and the freedom He secured for us through the cross and empty tomb.

I can't help but wonder if those who rejected Jesus and those who rejected Ann weren't cut from the same cloth.

Although it seems at times like critical voices are often the loudest, they are not the voices that should concern us. Don't ever buy into the lie that your gifts, abilities, and talents aren't good enough. You are God's workmanship, created in Christ Jesus (Ephesians 2:10). You are unlike any other, and we need each other's gifts. I need yours and you need mine (1 Corinthians chapter 12). So, I implore you…Grab your "drum" and march with me! And never stop asking, "Shall I play for Him?"

18 ~ CHRISTMAS MAGIC

JOHN ANDERSON

Christmas past, Christmas present, Christmas future – not really. Isn't it more like Christmas as a child, Christmas as a parent, and Christmas after the kids leave the house?

But Christmas anytime is magical, isn't it? Especially as a child. The lights on the tree, the presents, the family time, and the general goodness you can feel lingering in the air.

And then, we grow up (in some ways), have kids, and we want them to experience the Christmas we remember. We stay up late putting together toys, decorating the house, spending more than we can afford. Magical for them, yet for us exhausting, if not still magical.

Then in what seems like a sudden event, the kids are gone. Christmas is not as exhausting, nor as special. Once we were participants in all aspects, now we're relegated to the role of the observer: observing others caught up in the hustle and the bustle, observing others provide and experience that Christmas magic, while for us it feels somewhat like a fading memory.

But thankfully, things changed for me. A series of events or realizations happened over several years and the Christmas magic returned. To be honest… not just returned, but returned in a big way.

It began on the Christmas Eve I found myself in a store, in a mall, shopping for gifts and observing the Christmas crowds and scenes. I noticed a man with a child's bike hurrying to the checkout counter. He had a rumpled look; his hair mussed; his clothes were plain. I think I detected an air of hope and yet, at the same time, desperation.

I'm guessing what I saw was a sight we have all probably seen on one Christmas or another, but for me on this particular Christmas Eve, I had trouble not thinking about this scene. I wondered about his story: the story of this man, out by himself, buying a gift for a child so special to him.

Intrigued, I began contemplating. Was this gentleman struggling perhaps because of bad decisions, or through no fault of his own? Was his relationship with this child not where he had hoped and wanted it to be? Could it be he had visions that this Christmas was going to be different? An opportunity for him to shine again? Maybe his Christmas hope was for things to change, for his child to see him as the "Dad" he used to be or wanted to be again. I could almost see his child coming into the room and finding a bike with a big bow on it and feeling excited, feeling love and feeling his dad was 'that' guy again. This man, this dad, would probably be beaming, feeling so good, like times he remembered from better days, almost like life and their relationship were supposed to be.

So, based on this evidence, I reasoned Christmas might not be "too commercialized" as so often alleged. After all, could this man, in such a hurry on this Christmas Eve, needing something good to happen with his child, be able to create this anticipated experience in any other way, in this time frame? While admittedly any present, no matter how "perfect" will not provide the deep and lasting bond he probably yearned for, the type of bond only time and relationship can bring, it may be the sudden jolt needed to get things back on the right track. While his hope may have been to re-forge the bond with his child, buying this gift could be something quick, and even better, something he could do, and do immediately.

Fast forward a number of years. I had become a Christian and had been practicing my faith for quite some time, but something didn't feel quite right. I could remember experiencing a profound peace and joy in life that I truly believe came from God, but for some reason, now peace and joy were somewhat like a fading memory.

In my years as a Christian, I could not honestly say I had really changed very much at all. While having good intentions, I still had many of the same problems, still worried about all kinds of things daily, still got angry about things not worth getting angry about, still got offended by real or perceived slights, still had the same struggles with the same issues with more defeats than victories. I began to wonder, "Where is the evidence of the 'new life' the Bible seems to say I should have?"

I had reached the point where I needed something to change; I needed something different. With a mixture of hope and a bit of desperation I started searching more seriously, searching for truth. The Christianity I had lived wasn't working. I began reading and listening differently. I was searching for the type of truth that could change a person – and I mean *really change* them.

While on this journey, it started to sink in about how radical of a change this could be. I don't mean radical in the sense of huge life-changing decisions, but radical in the sense of changing my normal everyday (or every minute?) life.

After reading Matthew 5:5 that says, *"Blessed are the meek,"* I asked myself what would I do if I found myself in a position where I might have some advantage due to money, or power or something else, and not use that advantage because of me wanting to put others first?

Or, what if Philippians 4:6-7 really got hold of me? Worry seemed to be my default thinking, but what if God's *"Have no anxiety about anything, but in everything by prayer and supplication with thanksgiving, let your requests be made known to God and the peace of God which passes all understanding, will keep my mind and my heart in Christ Jesus"* became how I lived?

What would my life look like if I wasn't getting angry or offended about things I regularly got angry or offended about? This is the change I needed and was looking for.

It was obvious to me that to live this type of life took something I had not tapped into before and it would need to come from something outside of me. I think I had proven it with my past. It was clear to me this would not happen with the type of Christianity I was used to and had been living. But it was also clear to me this change was possible. I had seen it in others. I had glimpses of it in my life.

At some point in my search for the truth that could change my life, I remembered the man in a hurry from the Christmas Eve from years past. Like him, I was needing and wanting things to change, to be more like they were supposed to be. I decided I needed to do something outside of my comfort level and it needed to be something I could do and do now.

I made, what I considered, the *radical* decision to tithe.

In the past, I always had many, and what I thought were good, reasons why it just did not make sense to tithe. But I started tithing. It was a quick 'reset' or jump start for the type of change I needed.

It took a lot of faith and trust to do, but the results were incredible. It's hard to describe but it was something that happened almost immediately. If I had to use one word I would say, "freeing." I realized so many of my worries, frets, and sources of anger were somehow all related to money. And they kind of all just went away. It was almost like magic! I felt touched by God just by doing this, something I could do immediately. I probably felt like that child from years ago getting the bike from his Dad!

This was good. It helped me and helped me a lot, but there was more. To affect the change that I yearned required more. And the 'more' I needed was available - just as if God knew what I needed all along, although it took me all this time to discover it. Changing negative thoughts, actions and emotions that show up daily meant I needed daily help as well. After all, hadn't I proven to myself this was not something I was able to do with mere will power and good intentions?

And this is just what I found: the name Emanuel means 'God with you' and almost unbelievably, the God of the universe has provided us and me, with that power, the power of His presence within me whenever I need it. Wow! I had to keep asking myself if this is true. It turns out it is exactly what is promised. This is just what I had been looking for. Christ came with power to change my every day, even every minute of life in the way I wanted. I believed the journey that brought me to this point was a success!

But this begged a question. This power that I discovered, which God gives, must have been there all the time I was struggling and not moving forward in life.

In fact, it turns out God's presence in my daily life was available the whole time I needed it. I just didn't use it, did not even tap into it. Honestly, I didn't know how. So, for me, the first journey was ending but the next one was beginning. Now I'm continuing this journey, following where I believe the Lord is taking me. I'm learning the truth packed into Romans 12:2: *"Do not be conformed to this world but be transformed by the renewal of your mind, that you may prove what is the will of God, what is good and acceptable and perfect"* (RSV).

19 ~ OH, NO, NOT ANOTHER FRUITCAKE!

MARGERY KISBY WARDER

Fruitcake is one of those foods that you either hate or love with the first bite. Your relationship with fruitcake is not tied to bloodlines. Your feelings about fruitcake do not necessarily correspond to how much you like or dislike Christmas. And, though you may be forever haunted by the frozen stare you receive if you refuse a fruitcake, it does not mean you rejected the person who gave it to you. However, by consensus, let's admit that devout fruitcake lovers defy logic. Hear my case.

Mom was Swedish. The Swedish do not make fruitcake. They make fruit soup. They know the difference, or should. And Swedes claim they like sensible things - lutefisk and potato sausage and brown beans and herring - for Christmas.

What sane Swedish *flicka* would ever marry someone with whom her digestive system would collide?

But it happens. At least it did once and I lived to tell about it.

Third-generation English Dad courted first-generation Swedish Mom. When English Dad gave Swedish Mom his last name, she didn't realize it came steeped in plum pudding and fruitcake.

The English swear their allegiance to fruitcake with the same irrational fervor that Swedes swear allegiance to lutefisk.

How long would this marriage last under such "incompalatable" conditions?

Marital love makes compromising into an art. Love compelled a Swedish bride to help make English fruitcake and love made an English husband tolerate the smell and taste of lutefisk. Would the descendants of this cross-cultural couple adopt their Christmas compromise or would they wrinkle their noses at both fruitcake and lutefisk?

Yes, years ago, before I was a sugar crystal in Mom's eye, Mom first made fruitcake with Dad's mother and his sisters. Those English ladies claimed they knew the deep dark secrets of fruitcake. I don't know every ingredient stirred into their fruitcakes, but gradually Mom not only earned the right to chop ingredients, she discovered she could tolerate the taste.

Mom stuck with the annual multi-day process in her mother-in-law's kitchen until she, a Swede, could be trusted with the English recipe. When that older generation quit stoking ovens and bequeathed cook stoves to the next generation, Mom voluntarily continued making fruitcake in her own home.

Where, you might ask, was the sanity in that? Even after she could have used the busyness of raising four children as an excuse, Mom made fruitcake. Even in the war years, with rationing going on, Mom made fruitcake.

Fruitcake is expensive. Fruitcake requires planning ahead. It requires shopping and chopping and baking and binding and finding a shelf to hide it away.

We could have told Mom she didn't need to hide it away. We didn't care if she and Dad ate it all and left nothing for us kids. We didn't like it. And we didn't much like lutefisk either.

"You'll grow to like it," we were told. With so many other options about what we could grow to like, why must we learn to like fruitcake?

Tradition! Everyone eats fruitcake at Christmas. Tradition!

Tradition? This from the same parents who said, "If everyone else jumped off the Empire State building, would you?"

Year after year, beautiful, for it was that, fruitcake sat on the Christmas dessert table boasting of altered cherries and other assorted fruits, chopped nuts, and that really, really, disgusting stuff called citron. Citron sounded like the right name for a gas company or maybe for a far-flung planet to which Superman could fling the fruitcake.

Fruitcake made me shiver without tasting it.

So why, you ask, did the phone conversation I had with my sister this year go like this:

Me: Hey, guess what the first thing was that I baked in my new oven?

Sister: Cookies!

Me: Nope.

Sister: A roast!

Me: Nope. Guess again.

Sister: Nope, I'll never guess. Too many possibilities. What'd you make?

Me: Fruitcake.

Sister: Fruitcake? Fruitcake!

Me: Yep.

Sister: Fruitcake? Mom's recipe? The one we hated? The one with citron? The one that when she'd give it to me I'd put it away in some dark corner of the pantry so I could justify throwing it away when I found it months later? You made *that* fruitcake?

Me: No. Not Mom's recipe, but I made fruitcake.

Sister: Why?

So I told her the rest of the story.

See, last year as my husband and I were leaving the home of our very dear and close friends, they said to us, "Hey, wait a minute. We have something for you. We know you two really like fruitcake, so we brought you some from Texas!"

My husband and I love these people, but we to this day have no earthly idea of how they ever came up with any indication that we liked fruitcake. My husband disliked fruitcake as strongly as I did. But we politely smiled, not wanting to be the last one to catch onto their joke.

It wasn't a joke.

These friends had been driving back from Houston when they saw the sign for a famous Texas fruitcake and for some unknown, and we would contend, unfounded, reason, they thought of us. Maybe subconsciously it was the nuts on that billboard? Anyway they got it into their heads that they remembered we *loved* fruitcake! They told us they drove twenty miles out of their way to get to the famous bakery and buy us that little round tin of fruitcake that they were holding out for us to take.

Without looking at each other, we thanked them for their kindness and took the fruitcake to the car. Inside the car we said, in spontaneous unison, "Fruitcake? Whatever made them think *we* liked fruitcake? They have us mixed up with someone else!"

But we took the fruitcake home. Thankfully it was small. We opened the tin. Sure enough, there it sat with five or six pecans smiling back at us.

We do have a weakness for pecans. So that night, or the next day, we unwrapped the cellophane and got out a sharp knife and cut a teeny, tiny slice of fruitcake to sniff.

The sniff didn't gag us. In fact it kind of intrigued us, so we each nibbled on our piece.

Unbelievable! We *liked* the fruitcake. *That* fruitcake. *Only* that fruitcake. We more than liked it - we *loved* it!

Within a couple days, we divided the too-tiny fruitcake carefully and evenly. We ate the fruitcake and we carefully worded our thank you to our friends, not for remembering how much we liked fruitcake, but for giving us the fruitcake. We know they had us mixed up with someone else, but we're glad in the grand scheme of things that they thought we were the fruitcake lovers.

So this Christmas, when we debated what to give them, our closest friends, naturally we thought, "Fruitcake." People usually give a gift they wish would have been given to them, right?

We looked online and discovered that little round tin of fruitcake mistakenly given to us last year was a costly sacrifice we weren't sure we wanted to make. I'm not saying we're cheap or that we don't value our friends. I am saying I hope the price this year was higher than it was last year, and if you invested in that stock, you probably made out like a bandit!

Not wanting to part with my grandkids' tuition fund, I looked online to learn about fruitcakes. I also found a "like" recipe that claimed it imitated the Texas fruitcake we prized. I went for the "five star" recipe.

Christmas was approaching, so I toiled. I shopped and chopped and baked and wrapped loaves of fruitcake. Mine was mostly nuts held together by candied fruit and a tiny bit of cake. No citron. None.

I made nine small loaves. We ate the first one as a test. It passed.

We forced ourselves to give some loaves to friends, but we checked first to see if they were willing to try it. I mailed some to family, but only after I asked them to be truthful about whether they liked fruitcake. Most, unlike my sister, let silence slowly migrate down the phone line. Okay, since it was small and a palate-changer, they'd try it, but no promises.

I wasn't offended, at least not deep down. People have a thing about fruitcake. It's not an "eh" thing. It's not a wishy-washy thing. It's strong, like a, "Do you believe in capital punishment?" thing. It's almost always "No!" or "Yes!"

I decided to objectively research fruitcake, in person and on cold days, in my pajamas, online.

I heard and read fruitcake stories. I developed a thick skin so I could look at fruitcake cartoons.

I was grief-struck, but I understood how fruitcake could forever be held in disdain because an elderly woman, one, mind you, gave a weary, snow-shoveling impressionable youth a loaf of fruitcake instead of the eagerly anticipated gift or money. I could begin to even empathize, provided the fruitcake was loaded with citron. I'd even add my name to a petition to outlaw such un-Christmas gestures. Bah Humbug!

I enlisted my husband to help with research. He'd laughed his way through fruitcake episodes on television in years past. He'd seen fruitcake catapulted by contestants, flung in a fashion similar to the buffalo chip or cow pie contests. He found fruitcake used as doorstops, sandbags, bookends, and speed bumps. Someone apparently used a fruitcake as a base to hold up a Christmas tree.

I have a long fuse. I believe in our palatable rights, but let me warn you, I start to get a little rankled when I learn there's a total disregard for the potential of destroying a perfectly good fruitcake. I'm not sure whom you should answer to, but I'm sure you should answer to someone. I know I wasn't always like this, I didn't always hold this position, but as more evidence comes to light, to quote most flip-flopping politicians, I have a right to ask that you give little credence to my earlier positions. Especially when it comes to my evolving positions about fruitcake.

So, people hear me now. Hear me. See my fist raised toward the sky. Now I, like my English ancestors, boldly make the case for fruitcake. Fruitcake shall make a comeback. It shall become a tradition passed down through my descendants.

Why? Because fruitcake is good and because I made it, I mailed it, and I will, God-spare-my-life-till-next-Christmas, make it again! So eat it, my child, eat it! It's tradition!

The End

Editor's note: Check out the fruitcake recipe in another section.

20 ~ THE BABY CHRISTMAS TREE QUEST

CATHEY COOK

One year I really wanted two small artificial Christmas trees to put at our front door. Being the frugal person that I am, after seeing the price of the trees, I began to come up with a plan to get some trees, with a little help from our grandsons and my husband. Our property extends way back into the woods and having taken many walks there, I knew there were several big cedar trees scattered along the path. And where there are big trees, there are baby trees. I thought we could make this a fun project with the grandkids and have a way to get my trees also. We dubbed it, "The Baby Christmas Tree Quest."

I was teaching school at the time and would pick up the boys on Thursday afternoons in order to have some Mawmaw and Pawpaw time with them.

This afternoon we loaded up in the faithful Radio Flyer and took off to the woods. Of course, when the grandsons were this age, I was almost never without my camera. I have calmed down my "let me get the camera" instances somewhat since the grandchildren have grown older. Besides who wants pictures just of the backs of heads and hands!

As we trudged through layers of dried leaves, their crunch-crunch sound and the chatter of excited little voices reverberated through the trees. Such a sweet peaceful sound in an otherwise silent place. Thank you, Father, for peace and family!

As the "big" boys (although, a four-year old might not be considered big to some) did the shoveling and digging, our two-year old enjoyed playing with leaves and looking around in wonder of this huge place. He did look so small in the big expanse of woods. But sometimes one's job is just waiting.

We soon had the first step of the project completed. We loaded two nice-sized baby cedar trees and we were on our way!

When we arrived back at the house, both boys were excited to help with potting and watering the trees. I did the finishing work later, adding the bows, big candy canes, and lights.

I really did enjoy displaying those trees by the front door that season, but most of all I enjoyed the quest of finding them, watching Pawpaw and our oldest grandson digging them up, bringing them to the house, and having little hands help with the potting and watering of the trees we found on our "Baby Tree Quest." These were precious, precious times with our two oldest grandchildren. If you have little ones around, I encourage you to take the time (if at all possible) and share life with them. It's not just for them, but it is also for you!

Psalm 119:90 "Thy faithfulness is unto all generations: thou hast established the earth, and it abideth" (KJV).

21 ~ 101 WAYS TO SHOW LOVE

SALLY U. SMITH

The Christmas tree in the corner was fully decorated. We sat on the floor and enjoyed the lights. I picked up Heather, our infant, and went to the kitchen.

In her carrier, Heather watched each kernel of popcorn explode and bounce off the lid. While we munched on some buttery popcorn, my husband and I turned our attention to the empty area between the family room and the kitchen.

"I think the barn will fit there."

My husband Jerry placed his tape measure along the length and width of the small tent. "Yes, it will fit."

We covered three sides of the frame with sand-colored canvas. Then we glued a few pieces of straw on the roof. Jerry brought the nativity set from the garage.

"Steve, the mother's name is Mary," I said.

"Maey," said our three-year-old.

Jerry added, "The father is named Joseph."

Heather waved her hands. Jerry placed the manger between them and aimed a spot light on the open side of the barn.

"Why do these people live in a barn?"

"They don't, Steve. They were on a trip and couldn't find a place to stay. A kind man let them sleep in his warm and dry barn," I said.

My husband placed the animals in the barn.

"Did they sleep with a cow and a sheep?"

"And one of these," said Jerry.

"A donkeyyy." Steve crawled into the barn and lay between the cow and a lamb.

"Mary and Joseph had a baby boy named Jesus. He will grow up to be someone special. Someone famous," said Dad.

I started some Christmas music on the stereo system. "Steve, we need to make a bed for Baby Jesus. We are going to use the feed box."

Jerry added some straw in the bottom.

"Steve, we don't want Jesus to get scratched. Go to your bedroom and bring our very best baby blanket."

Steve dashed to the bedroom and brought me his 101 Dalmatians blanket. He helped me wrap and place Jesus in his bed.

As we hummed, "Away in a Manger," Jerry and I beamed at each other.

(Editor's Note: If you have a little one who would like to hear and watch the "Away in the Manger" song as it's played on YouTube, here is another possible version for your enjoyment: https://www.youtube.com/watch?v=1YXvhbX0m-Q)

22 ~ THE LITTLE THINGS

JANIS LUSSMYER

We waited upstairs in eager anticipation. Mom had written the annual reminder to Santa that our family opened gifts on Christmas Eve, so he needed to stop at our house first. When I was six, I wondered and worried how he would enter our house because we had no chimney. Would he come in the front door or magically squeeze himself down the vent pipe from the roof? In a moment of sheer relief, I remembered we were celebrating at Grandpa's house, and he had a chimney so Santa could arrive the way he was supposed to.

Each year, Mom told us to wait for the jingle bells. Their sound was the signal that Santa was departing. Once we heard the jingle-jangle, we rushed down the stairs; all four of us jumbled together trying to be first. Many years later, I learned her secret: a leather strap of bells shaken hard and then tossed under the couch.

Before the gift-giving, Grandpa would read the Christmas story from his well-worn black leather Bible. After he died, Mom took over that tradition. We all were probably squirming in anticipation, but I loved imagining the angels and the shepherds and sweet baby Jesus all wrapped up in the manger.

We took turns pulling out gifts from under the tree. The rule was not to look or try for any particular package. Then we would take the package to Mom, who would read the tag, and we would excitedly, yet solemnly, deliver the gift to the recipient. Finally, we would all watch while the gift was opened and thanks and hugs were shared.

On what turned out to be Grandpa's last Christmas, I received the gift of my dreams from Mom: a china tea set. Looking back, I am quite sure that Grandpa must have supplied the Santa gifts that year because Mom had only a dollar to spend for each of us children. I still have that tea set— well, most of the pieces have survived these 55 years. I remember having tea parties when Mom would let me use real tea and milk and sugar, which all tasted extra good in that tea set.

So often it is the little things in life that end up meaning the most. What little things can we do or say or share this Christmas to communicate the life-changing love of our Savior?

23 ~ OUR FIRST CHRISTMAS
DEANNA KAHRE

It is Christmas Eve. The Christmas program is over and everyone has gone home. We are downstairs in the children's opening area. You sit on a miniature chair and I sit on one of the tables. With some teasing, we exchange gifts.

You have given me a card, something I haven't thought to give you. That makes me feel special. I open the card and read it. After telling you, thank you for the card, I open the box. Inside is a small container of Yuka perfume. The label says "Perfumes of the Desert." The lettering is arched over a Yuka plant. I set it aside and concentrate on the next item. It is wrapped in paper. Carefully I pull back the paper to reveal a six-inch pot that is off-white with a design of rust and black.

"It is made by the Indians in New Mexico," you explain.

"I love it!" I reply.

You open your gift next. It is a reversible belt. You say, "This is just what I needed."

"I just hope it fits," I reply, laughing nervously. We visit a bit longer and then part with a hug.

Years later you will tell me you really hadn't known what to get me, but you didn't invest in a bigger gift because you didn't know if our relationship was going to last.

Thirty-eight years later we are still helping with Christmas programs and exchanging gifts.

24 ~ A YULETIDE WEDDING PROPOSAL

CODY HALL

I first remember spending time with Emily in a season of the year far-removed from Christmas. I was an intern with an engineering ministry in Indiana, and they were having a 4th of July outing at a county park for the staff and their families. Emily's father also worked at the ministry, and Emily attended the event with her father and mother.

I only remember saying a few words to her that day and thinking, "Hmm, she's pretty cool." I did not consider her anything more than an acquaintance after that day. Even after I started attending her church and joined her Sunday School class, nothing past feelings of friendship developed in my heart toward her.

This was in 2013. The year finished with us remaining friends, but *acquaintances* is probably a more accurate word. I could count on one hand the number of conversations we had with each other. They were not memorable; just normal things people say to each other while hanging out with friends in groups.

Sometime early in 2014, she began getting serious with a long-distance boyfriend she had known since childhood. I continued to think of her as only a friend, and in the back of my mind, her "taken" status reinforced that. During the summer she got engaged to her boyfriend. I remember thinking, "Oh, that's good for her!"

Her engagement, however, was short-lived. The relationship fell apart, and Emily went through a difficult personal time. From the outside looking in, she didn't seem too affected by it. She seemed to handle it well. Knowing her as my dear wife now, it was much more difficult than she let on.

In November of 2014, the ministry appointed me to missionary service. This meant that I could go out and raise support to become one of their full-time missionary engineers. I returned to West Virginia where I grew up and began working full-time while raising support. I met with individuals, visited and spoke in churches, and took several intentional support raising trips to areas where I knew many people.

God blessed my support raising tremendously. It was a time of growth for me in every area of my life. Spiritually, my faith in God grew as I saw Him provide. Mentally, my long-term thinking and planning grew as I thought about my future in ministry. Relationally, I grew to love and value people more, not because of what I could get out of them, but because God had created them in His image!

After fifteen months of raising support, God allowed me to reach one hundred percent. I returned to Elkhart in April of 2016 to begin work. The Sunday School class had been meeting each Monday night for Bible study and I attended the gathering my first week back. I remember seeing Emily there, and thinking, "Oh, wow, there's Emily." Something was different, but I didn't know what. I decided I needed to start talking to her and get to know her more.

One night a couple weeks later after a church softball game, I went out to eat with two of my teammates who were and are still close friends of mine. They were also part of our Sunday School class and friend group. I told them, "Guys, I think I'm going to ask Emily out." They were completely supportive and we talked more about it. I told them something had changed and I was interested in her.

I decided to try talking with her intentionally for a couple of weeks; I wanted to see if I could read her interest level. I knew I would be able to tell if she was open to getting to know me better, or if she didn't care at all about me!

I was only seeing her twice a week: once at church, and once at Bible study on Monday nights. I found a way to plug myself into whatever conversation she was having with others, and eventually it would be only she and I talking together! We had great conversations. Nothing too deep, but enough to let me see that she was at least comfortable talking to me. She never told me to go away, so I knew there was a chance!

I did go away, though, near the end of April. In New York I participated in a week-long mission conference at a church there. When I returned, I decided to ask Emily out the next time I saw her, which would have been the next Sunday.

That Sunday also happened to be Mother's Day. Emily left Sunday School early to spend time with her mother and grandmother. Hmm. That left the next day after Bible study as the big night when I would ask her to coffee.

We enjoyed Bible study with our friend group as always. As it ended, I made sure we walked outside together. Emily must have known I was going to ask something, because she made a beeline for her car! I quickly got around in front of her (in a non-threatening way!) and said something like, "Hold on a second, I have something I want to ask you. Will you go get a coffee with me tomorrow night?"

Emily responded with: "I guess so, but don't tell anybody."

Imagine the different emotions I felt upon hearing that! Happiness because she said yes, but curiosity and surprise that she did not want anyone to know about it! Emily does not like drama or being the center of attention, so naturally she wanted our outing to be kept between us. She knew that once people there at work found out we had gone out, they would start talking and before long, …well, it was just best, she thought, to hide my asking her out for coffee.

I agreed to her condition. I was simply thankful she said, "Yes."

The next day we met to talk at a local coffee shop. Emily got an unsweetened tea, so I gave her a hard time. I'm from the south and we like our tea sweet. I had a coffee. By the end of our time, she had hardly sipped her tea. Months later, she told me that she had been nervous, but I could hardly tell it! Our conversation flowed easily.

In the coming weeks we continued going out and spending time together. People started hearing about our relationship, so it became official. Things progressed well, and we loved getting to know each other more deeply.

In my mind, I had established a timeline: six months dating, and six months engaged. Of course, I did not mention this to Emily for several months. I didn't want to scare her off!

All summer and fall, I purchased what I needed to remodel my home and I was glad to have Emily's help while I worked on the house. However, remodeling costs meant I didn't have much extra cash to set aside for an engagement ring, but I saved what I could as quickly as I could. During our times together, we talked more and more about our views on marriage and we began talking about the possibility of marrying each other.

After many discussions, I talked to Emily's father and got his permission to marry her. Emily and I were still just dating, but we decided to begin premarital counseling with our pastor. We knew the counseling material was lengthy, so we didn't want to wait until we were engaged to start it. We didn't want to cram all the counseling sessions into too small of a time window.

Counseling with our pastor began and progressed well. I needed to start planning how I would make my proposal of marriage to Emily. Winter had arrived and I knew Emily enjoyed going to look at Christmas light displays on homes and in parks. Somehow I would incorporate the light displays into my proposal. I began to think about how to make some sort of sign out of Christmas lights. I also started looking for neighborhoods whose residents put on light displays.

After a couple of weeks of planning, I decided to use rope lights and plywood to make a sign spelling out my big question! I drilled holes in the plywood in the proper locations so that when the rope lights were strung through the holes, they formed letters that spelled, "Will you marry me?" I painted the plywood sections white so the lights would be brighter and I threaded the lights through the holes. It worked! My sign was complete. Now I just needed to find somewhere to take Emily so I could pop the question.

After more research on locations, I realized a neighborhood in a nearby town puts on an incredible annual Christmas light display. The residents decorate their houses, yards, and just about everything else that's visible from the street. That sounded perfect. I drove over to the neighborhood one evening after work to see if there was a house with a layout that would lend itself well to my mission.

My plan was to meet the homeowners, describe what I wanted to do, and see if they would let me set up in their yard! I drove all around the neighborhood, and didn't see any houses that made sense for my situation. I was about to give up when, at the end of one the last cul-de-sacs, I saw *the* house!

This house was one of the largest in the neighborhood, but it had a modest and elegant light display in the front yard. What caught my eye was a manger scene set up in the center of the yard in front of a tree. Above the manger, a lighted sign said; "Wise men still seek Him." I thought, "This is the house."

I got out of my car and walked up to the front door to knock on it and introduce myself to the homeowners. After knocking two times over a couple of minutes, I decided they must not be home. I turned and walked back across the yard toward my car.

When I got about halfway to the road, a car pulled up and around the cul-de-sac. It stopped in front of the mailbox. A man rolled down his window to get his mail out, saw me, and asked if he could help me. I cordially introduced myself and explained what I was doing there. I mentioned that their manger display with the lighted sign had caught my eye and wondered if they would allow me to use their yard to propose to my girlfriend.

They were excited and very positive toward the idea! We exchanged phone numbers. I assured them I would be in touch over the next couple of days so I could arrange to go over and set up my signage.

Meantime, I discovered it was hard work trying to cover my tracks and explain to Emily what I had been up to for the last couple of days. It didn't help that I underestimated the time it would take to transport everything over to the "engagement" house to try to set it up exactly where I thought it needed to be. All that setting up made me late to something the next day. I tried to come up with some generic excuse and Emily seemed to buy it!

Along about this time, I made plans with Emily that her parents would join us that Friday night while we drove around area neighborhoods to see the Christmas lights. She was excited about the double date, and so was I!

I explained everything to her father. He agreed to help me by agreeing to take some pictures and doing what he could to make sure we didn't run into any snags.

The day before the big double date, I set everything up on the property. I arranged the sign in a partial circle, not visible from the road, so a person would have to walk up to the front door of the house and turn around before the sign could be seen or read. I told the homeowner I would warn him when we were about five minutes away so he could go out and pretend to be shoveling snow or doing something else outside not far from the front door. Seeing him would give me an excuse to stop and get out and talk with him. My plan was to say something like this to Emily, "Hey, there's a guy I know that I'd really like you to meet!" I was sure that would get her out of the car and up to the front door.

The next day, I could not focus on anything at work. All I thought about was making sure things went smooth that night! I was quite nervous. I told my parents about my plans, and they were ecstatic. I made plans to call them when we entered the neighborhood with the light display, but, of course, I would keep my phone hidden so they could overhear the conversation, and hopefully the proposal.

After work, I drove to Emily's home and picked up everyone. Emily's father brought along his camera to "take pictures of the lights." He and I knew he planned to take pictures of other things too!

When we got into the neighborhood known for its lighted displays, I gave Emily printed directions showing all the streets so she could make sure we didn't miss any houses. I wanted to keep her busy with something so she didn't get suspicious. I even acted like I was lost a couple of times, which helped to cover my tracks.

I notified the homeowner according to my plan. Sure enough, as we approached the house, he was out on his sidewalk pretending to shovel snow. Picture perfect. Just as I'd hoped.

Sometimes when people get nervous they say they have butterflies in their stomach. I thought the ones I was experiencing were extinct. It felt like I had pterodactyls in my stomach!

I told Emily, "Oh, there's a guy I know! We should stop a minute so you can meet him."

I pulled into the driveway and put the car in park. This was the moment of truth! I needed her to get out of the car! Remember, it's cold December and we're in snowy Indiana. It took a little encouragement, but she got out of the car. Her father encouraged Emily's mother to get out as well, but she was more reluctant. He quietly told her, "Get out the car, and don't say anything!"

So there we were. All of us out of the car. We started walking down the sidewalk toward the front door where my new "old" friend was standing. He called out, maybe a little too loudly, "Hey, great to see you! How's it going?"

I responded with something, and then the homeowner's wife came out of the front door and walked toward us exclaiming, "Oh! Congratulations!" I was dumbfounded! She gave Emily a hug and then quickly followed that with an, "Oh…I mean, … I don't know what for!"

Emily, remember, doesn't like drama or being the center of attention. For all she knew, these brand new acquaintances were a little too enthusiastic at meeting her! Emily seemed a little uncertain about what was going on.

Meanwhile my mind was going crazy!

The man's wife had all but spoiled the surprise! We were still a few steps away from where we needed to be before I could turn Emily around to have her see my sign. I put my arm behind Emily and gently started walking toward the front door to encourage Emily's movement toward the spot. I said something to the couple about going inside to visit with them for a minute.

As we got to my carefully planned turning point I stopped walking and Emily stopped with me. I took Emily's arm and said, "I want you to see something over here."

The look on her face told me she was grasping what was going on. I said, "Let's walk over here a minute." We walked a few steps through the snow to a spot I had cleared earlier. The sign was now in full view, and she was taking it in.

I took her hands in mine, looked her in the eyes, and said, "Emily, to me you are a novel in a sea of magazines, a mountain in a world of hills. You're an ocean and all others are just duck ponds. Because of you, and God bringing us together, these last seven months have been the best of my life. I want to spend the rest of my life with you." I then got down on one knee and asked, "Emily Joan Anderson, will you marry me?"

She said yes, I slipped the ring on her finger, and stood up to hug her. She asked, "Are your knees shaking?" and I replied, "Yes! It's cold out here!"

THE END

25 ~ OUR FAMILY'S ADVENT DEVOTIONAL TIMES

MARY RUTH STEGER

The liturgical seasons of Advent and Christmas were a very significant part of my parents' preparation and celebration of the birth of the Christ Child. They were both living examples fit for instilling in us, their three children, "The Real Reason for the Season!"

My father was a Lutheran pastor who loved the Lord, so in our home, a devotional reading and prayer time always followed our evening meal. During the four weeks prior to Christmas, we celebrated Advent, a month-long season so rich in the history and symbolism of Christ, our Savior.

Like others whose family came from Norway, we used an evergreen Advent wreath to symbolize the eternal life Jesus came to offer sinners who believed in Him as Savior and Lord. Our wreath required five candles, and we were reminded Jesus came as the Light for a world lost in darkness.

Circling the evergreen wreath were four candles. For the readings of the first week, only one purple candle was lit. During our Bible reading and prayer time the second week, we were reminded of Israel's hope and longing for their promised Redeemer as our two purple candles burned.

On the third week, we lit the third purple candle, and by the last week before Christmas, we eagerly lit the pink candle. We all knew that candle as the "Joy" candle. My father likely selected the scriptures about the angel's visit to announce to Virgin Mary that she would give birth to God's Son, about Mary's visit to Elizabeth who was carrying John the Baptist and Elizabeth's baby leaped in her womb at the sound of Mary's voice. We also heard about Joseph being told in a dream that the child Mary would birth was God's Son and Joseph should take Mary to be his wife and name her child, Jesus.

The anticipation of celebrating Christmas had been building for four weeks. Only one candle sat unlit as we finished our Bible and prayer times on Christmas Eve.

Christmas Eve was always the Sunday School Christmas program at our church: singing Christmas carols, we each had a memorized "piece" to recite, and, of course, a live manger scene. I was usually "Mother Mary." I wonder why?

Inside the evergreen wreath was the white "Christ" candle that we eagerly and joyfully lit on Christmas Day to celebrate the birth of our Savior in Bethlehem. God had kept His promise. He had sent mankind's Redeemer and Mary and Joseph named Him, Jesus, just as they had been told to do.

Of course, during Advent all the candle lighting and flickering flames fascinated us children. Like other Norwegian children, we sometimes had a tug-of-war to see who would light the proper candles before the devotional readings and prayer, and who would have the privilege of putting out the flames when the last "Amen" was said. That still happens in homes today during the lighting of the Advent candles and we've seen it with our own children and grandchildren. Maybe they try to come up with different solutions, like we did, to see who would win!

Another fun part of Christmas for me as a young child was hanging my decorated Christmas stocking on a doorknob for Santa to fill when he came to our house during the night. On Christmas morning I found the stocking filled with apples, oranges, popcorn, and peanuts.

Some families traveled to be with relatives at Christmas. We were always at home, as my father was pastor of three small town Lutheran congregations in Wisconsin and South Dakota, where he was needed to "shepherd his flock."

We pray that these meaningful Advent traditions will continue with future generations of the Scobey-Steger families, and perhaps other families will choose to follow them, too.

JOY TO THE WORLD, THE LORD HAS COME! HALLELUJAH!

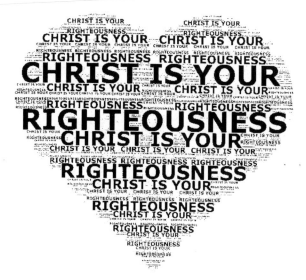

26 ~ BECAUSE OF JESUS, I ...

JEAN NELSON

Jesus answered him, "Truly, truly, I say to you, unless one is born anew, he cannot see the kingdom of God." Nicodemus said to Him, "How can a man be born when he is old? Can he enter a second time into his mother's womb and be born?" (John 3:3-4 RSV)

Early in the 1970s, I sat with a cluster of gals from my extended family, enjoying our usual light bantering back and forth until Deloris told us we needed to be born again. What a strange term to drop into an otherwise pleasant conversation. Deloris was serious. She'd just returned from a Billy Graham Crusade and had been taught from the Gospel of John about being born again.

I didn't know much of the Bible. When I later read from John 3 in the Holy Bible, it came as no surprise to me that Nicodemus would ask Jesus the same question I asked Deloris that day: "How can I go back into my mother's womb to be born again?"

Her comment stunned me. Obviously we had all been born once, but what did it mean to be born "again" and who did Deloris, or Billy Graham for that matter, think they were to tell us we needed to be born again, to change our status? I was offended. I was trying to be a good wife to Donnie, a loving mother to my children, and I lived responsibly in society – how could anyone imply I wasn't a "Christian" person?

I'm pretty sure Deloris answered my question and told us Jesus Christ had said, *"Except a man be born again, he cannot see the kingdom of God,"* but I was so angry I didn't hear or understand anything Deloris said. She probably went home thinking she had failed. She probably thought she had wasted her words on our little group. She likely felt embarrassed.

Maybe Deloris questioned whether the Holy Spirit had prompted her to speak or if she'd charged ahead on her own. I think the Holy Spirit did play a role in that conversation because, though I was angry, try as I would to disregard Deloris's statement, I couldn't ever fully dismiss her words.

I couldn't have known it at the time, but God was keeping His promise. He said, *"So shall my word be that goeth forth out of my mouth: it shall not return unto me void, but it shall accomplish that which I please, and it shall prosper in the thing whereto I sent it"(Isaiah 55:11 KJV)* ...even if the listener gets angry and offended and claims the messenger sounds pious and judgmental.

For the next thirty years I went about raising my daughters and being a wife to Donnie, the man I'd married in the Red Oak (Iowa) Methodist Church. My husband owned Nelson Dairy and partly because of his schedule, we were not a church-going family.

When we were asked if we wanted to be removed from the membership roll, we said, "Sure, that would be fine."

A few years later, Donnie sold his business and worked for Anderson-

Erickson Dairy. Against my wishes, Donnie agreed to move us to the Kansas City area just after our first granddaughter was born. Also, he had been diagnosed with COPD. 1991 became a difficult year of adjustments.

We grandmothers need our "grandchildren fix," so I was pleased when Donnie agreed to let me spend a few days around Christmas with my daughter's family in Iowa. What a treat that time was going to be – back with family and all that was familiar. I looked forward to the busyness of the Christmas season, but while there, I opted to cross off one more thing on my "to do" list by having my yearly mammogram while back in Red Oak.

Three days before Christmas, when I should have been mostly concerned about fussing over my granddaughter and family, I learned I needed to have a follow-up biopsy. Many times that happens after a mammogram and life moves on. So, the day after Christmas the biopsy was performed.

On New Year's Eve, the call about the biopsy report came. I had breast cancer. Less than a week later, I started the "New Year" with my mastectomy. A few weeks later, I began chemotherapy back in Missouri.

I finished my chemo in September, but we realized Donnie's health had completely failed. God had our attention. Donnie agreed we could start going to church. What a joy it was for us to become active in a church not far from where we lived, Grover Park Baptist.

Donnie's health continued to deteriorate. He took early retirement in 1993. We gradually took steps in 1994 that brought us to our Red Oak house on our thirty-fourth wedding anniversary. For months I witnessed the way COPD ravages a person's body and the way it contributes to tense interactions that can embroil couples and family members. Sadly, my husband and I became angry strangers.

During this turmoil, I joined the Presbyterian Church. Donnie could only do so by proxy because of his health. Thankfully, as father of the bride, he could walk our daughter down the aisle on her lovely wedding day in which two of our grandchildren also participated.

The next month, my husband was hospitalized. We were prepared to have him treated for COPD and chronic bronchitis. Instead, we were shocked to hear the devastating news that Donnie's COPD had become end-stage emphysema. My husband was losing his life and that chapter of our lives was closing. Soon our children and grandchildren had to journey on through life without Dad and Grandpa. Disease is such a horrible curse in our world.

After my cancer diagnosis and Donnie's death, I began to long for more spiritual answers. I read Tim LaHaye's intriguing "Left Behind" series. In February 2000, I accepted an invitation to join our local chapter of Community Bible Study.

Can you guess the topic of the Bible study? John 3 - when Nicodemus asks Jesus how anyone can be born again.

I began to understand what Deloris had told me thirty years before. By God's mercy and grace, I can report that seventeen years ago I became born again! I am so thankful God never quit drawing me to Him.

Before long, I started attending Grace Baptist Church, was baptized by immersion, became active in Bible camps and began using my singing talents in ministry, which I praise the Lord I have been able to continue to do each week at a local nursing home. I am so thankful I am now a Child of God!

How foolish of me to have thought I could get to heaven by being good. In Ephesians chapter two, verses eight and nine, we read: *"For by grace are ye saved through faith; and that not of yourselves: it is the gift of God: Not of works, lest any man should boast" (KJV)*.

Humbly, I had to admit I was a sinner in need of a Savior.

Christmas is a great time to let others know I am so thankful my Savior left Heaven to come to Bethlehem to die on Calvary for my sins. I am grateful that humble shepherds, adventurous wise men, courageous disciples, and faithful believers, including people like Deloris, kept passing the Good News of Jesus down through the ages so that when my heart was humble enough to listen to God's invitation to be saved, I could respond in faith.

I was a lost sinner, but because of Jesus, I am now a Child of God. My favorite Bible verse has become John 3:7: *"Ye must be born again."* Jesus was so loving when He told us sinners how we could become new creatures and I eagerly tell those I love this truth because I don't want to miss spending eternity without them nearby. I know when this earthly body takes in its last breath I shall be with the Lord for eternity!

Who knows? Maybe I'm a bit like Deloris. Regardless, I'm so thankful Deloris's unwelcome comment initiated my awareness of my need for salvation, for a change in my eternal destination. Certainly, I do not know when my final earth day will come. I have unexpectedly lost family and friends dear to me, which saddens me because I will miss them. Each death reminds me there is no guarantee about how much time any of us has left to live on earth. We have no guarantees we can decide "later" about trusting only Jesus Christ for our salvation. God said it plainly in Acts 16:31 (KJV): *Believe on the Lord Jesus Christ, and thou shalt be saved.*

I do know I intend to serve God as faithfully as I know how each day I draw in breath. I also know I can fearlessly face daily life, and death, knowing Heaven is just a breath away. I am not righteous and worthy on my own. Jesus' life, death and resurrection demonstrate God's mercy and grace is available to each of us who trust Jesus Christ as our only way into the eternal presence of God.

Because of Jesus and my "second birth" seventeen years ago, my life changed. Things of God became more important to me. Today I appreciate Christian radio, my pastor's teachings, fellowship with other Christians as we study God's Word, using my gifts for God's glory, and, of course, speaking with my Heavenly Father in prayer. I have seen God's gracious care of me when cancer did not defeat my body. Recently, I could have been killed in a car accident; even after narrowly surviving that, when I took the car in for its post-accident check-up, mechanics discovered the left front lug-nut was cracked, which only reaffirmed that merciful God's plans for my life were not over. I have known the assurance of God's love for my little grandchildren whom I did not get to hold.

I have been the recipient of the Lord's tender mercies time after time, and when life has been difficult, I have known He was with me.

In 2012 I was thrilled to take a "once in a lifetime" trip to Israel that let me be in the region where Jesus had lived and died before His resurrection and ascension. As wonderful as that trip was, better still is the confidence I have that because of God's grace and my faith, I will spend eternity in heaven. Will you? I hope so.

Listen, reader friend. Hear the love in God's words when He says, *"For God so loved the world, that he gave His only begotten Son, that whosoever believeth in him should not perish, but have everlasting life. For God sent not his Son into the world to condemn the world; but that the world through him might be saved" (John 3:16-17, KJV).*

Recipes

Oh, taste and see that the Lord is good...

Psalm 34:8

27 ~ MARILYN'S BREAKFAST CASSEROLE

Marilyn Boone

6 slices of bread   1 pound roll of sausage
2 cups (8 ounces) grated cheddar cheese
8 eggs   2 cups milk
1 tsp. dry mustard   1 tsp. salt

Cut bread into small cubes and layer in bottom of a 9x13 baking dish. Brown and drain sausage then layer on top of the bread. Sprinkle cheddar cheese over the top. In a bowl, whisk together eggs, milk, dry mustard and salt. Pour evenly over layers in dish. Cover and refrigerate overnight. Bake at 350 degrees for 35 minutes or until lightly browned and center is done.

28 ~ CHRISTMAS MORNING ROLLS

Marilyn Boone

1 package frozen dinner rolls (about 24)
1 box dry butterscotch pudding (for cooked, not instant)
1 stick butter   3/4 cup brown sugar
3/4 tsp. cinnamon   1/2 cup chopped pecans

Arrange frozen rolls in greased Bundt pan. Sprinkle dry pudding over rolls. In saucepan, stir butter, sugar and cinnamon over medium heat, just until sugar is dissolved and the mixture comes to a boil. Pour evenly over rolls. Sprinkle with nuts. Cover tightly with foil or plastic wrap. Let set on countertop overnight. The next morning, remove the cover and bake at 350 degrees for 30 minutes. Let stand a couple of minutes before inverting onto plate, scraping out any remaining topping.

29 ~ CATHEY'S BREAKFAST CASSEROLE

One pound bulk sausage (hot or mild)
3 cups frozen hashbrown potatoes, thawed
1/4 to 1/2 tsp. salt
3 cups (12 oz.,) shredded cheddar cheese (I prefer sharp)
1/2 chopped green peppers
12 eggs beaten

2 cups milk

1. Cook the sausage, crumble and drain.
2. Place hashbrowns in lightly greased 13 x 9 x 2 inch baking dish.
3. Sprinkle with salt.
4. Layer sausage, cheese and green peppers.
5. Combine eggs and milk, stirring well and pour over peppers.
Bake in a preheated oven at 350 for approximately 50 minutes.
Serves 8-10.

Cathey Cook says, "The 'Breakfast Casserole' is so nice during the holiday season, especially if you have a group to feed. You can put it together the night before and pop it into the oven in the morning while you are enjoying overnight company or while doing last minute preparations for some holiday affair. I have also made the casserole as a snack for our early Sunday School class. It is so easy and very versatile. I hope you enjoy it.

30 ~ CATHEY'S CHRISTMAS SAUSAGE QUICHE

"This is our traditional Christmas breakfast now that there are only 3 adults in the house for Christmas morning," says Cathey.

1 9-inch deep-dish pie shell
½ pound sausage   1 1/2 cup grated cheddar cheese (mild or sharp)
1 small onion grated (or ½ Tbsp. minced dried onion)
1 Tbsp. flour   1 large can evaporated milk (12 oz.)
2 eggs   parsley

1. Brown sausage in a skillet over medium heat and drain.
2. Place sausage in the pie shell and sprinkle with grated cheese, flour, and onion.
3. Beat eggs and milk.
4. Pour over the sausage and cheese.
5. Sprinkle parsley on top and bake in a preheated oven at 350 for 45 minutes or until set.

(Ed. Note: Cathey has a cookbook or two online...and blogs recipes, too. See her bio in the back of this book.)

31 ~ OH, YES! TRY THIS FRUITCAKE!

Margery Kisby Warder

PLAN AHEAD - I suggest "little" loaf or round baking pans. They'll be good "fresh," but best to bake, cool, wrap, store…if you can.

24 ounces pitted dates   1 lb. candied pineapple (cut into chunks)
1 lb. candied red and green cherries (sticky kind in little containers)
2 cups sifted **all-purpose** flour   2 teaspoons baking powder
1/2 teaspoon salt   4 eggs
½ cup white sugar, granulated   ½ cup brown sugar, packed
8 cups of nuts – (pecans and/or walnuts to get eight total cups for inside the fruitcake.)

Plan to garnish loaves with pecan halves around candied cherries and brush the top of each loaf with light corn syrup before storing.

Preheat oven to 275 degrees F. Grease two (9 by 5 by 3-inch) loaf pans with butter; line with parchment paper; lightly grease paper.

Put dates, pineapple and cherries in large bowl. Add flour, baking powder, and salt in sifter and sift onto fruit. Mix well with hands until well coated. Set aside.

Beat eggs until frothy; gradually beat in sugar. Add to the chopped fruit and mix well with large wooden spoon. Add nuts and mix with hands until everything is well coated.

Pack into prepared pan(s) pressing with palms of hands.

Bake in a 275 degree Fahrenheit oven – larger loaves for 1 1/2 hours or tube pan for 1 1/4 hours. Check earlier for smaller loaves. Remove from oven. Let stand on a cooling rack 5 minutes. Turn out. Peel paper off. Turn top side up and, if desired, brush with light corn syrup. Cool. Wrap loosely in foil. Store in airtight container in cool place, up to several weeks…if you can ignore the loaves that long as they "ripen."

IF YOU WANT TO "SAVE" THE FRUITCAKE …. Freeze before wrapping well to store in freezer. Some say these could actually last over a year, but is that accurate? I suspect it's not likely many who taste the cakes would intentionally plan on keeping theirs that long.

You know, of course, the faster method is to place an order with your favorite fruitcake supplier. They are the proven experts. Just saying. ☺

32 ~ MARILYN SEYMOUR'S SWEDISH BROWN BEANS

2 20 oz. cans kidney beans

½ c. brown sugar

6 Tbsp. finely cut bacon

¼ tsp. cinnamon

1 or 2 Tbsp. vinegar

Salt and pepper to taste

Simmer to reduce liquid and blend flavors and heat through. Serves 8.

33 ~ SWEDISH MEATBALLS LIKE GRANDMA'S & MOM's...
...ACCORDING TO MARGERY KISBY WARDER

2 lbs. lean hamburger   1 lb. pork sausage – "medium" or "mild"

1 onion, chopped (medium or large)   Salt and pepper

Mix the two meats with your hands; add the chopped onion and seasonings. Scoop out the mixture and roll in palm of your hands so each is somewhat firmly packed and walnut-size. Put into heavy skillet fairly close together because they "cook down" as fat leaves them. On "medium," slowly brown until crisp, but not burnt. Check the center of one to be sure it's cooked through. Keep them warm until serving them.

OPTIONAL GRAVY

Remove all but two of the cooked and crisp meatballs from the skillet – crumble those so everybody gets some in their gravy! ☺

Now in a jar with a tight lid, stir together 1 heaping teaspoon of cornstarch and 1 cup of milk or cream. Tighten the lid and shake the jar until the mixture looks smooth.

Gradually add this mixture into the very warm drippings you preserved (about 2 tablespoons 'grease' and the two crumbled meatballs), stirring so it all gets worked in together. Add one can, undiluted, Campbell's mushroom soup (your choice – beefy or regular and without MSG is a good idea). Stir until it all simmers for a couple minutes. Gravy usually changes color slightly when all its ingredients are heated through. Keep it warm on very low once it's the taste you want (adjust seasoning if needed). After the family says grace, ☺, offer the hot gravy for mashed potatoes and the meatballs, too. *Thickness varies; expand this by using more drippings, more milk/cream, and more undiluted soup.*

34 ~ MARGERY'S SWEDISH PANCAKES

Gradually mix together: 1 tablespoon melted butter, 1 cup of milk or cream, 3 eggs added one at a time, then 3/4 cup white sugar. Finally slowly add 1 cup flour. Batter will be thin and sweet.

Butter the skillet lightly and pour a "serving" into the hot skillet, tipping the small skillet to get the batter evenly distributed, circular, and thin. *Adjust temperature as needed – stoves and skillets vary.* Let batter "set' slightly, then flip it over carefully to brown slightly on the second side. Serve with the Scandinavian lingonberries or with raspberry or other preserves. Some sprinkle with powdered sugar or top with whipped cream before serving, or add a few whole berries as garnish.

ALSO, you can fill these pancakes with a sweetened cream cheese or cream cheese and coconut or fill them with a thick chocolate sauce mixture and roll them and garnish as a dessert.

If you don't want to stand and do each one individually, these work on a griddle, and can be tipped to cover the whole griddle, but then cut the pancake as it sets into the size you want to flip over. I like the pancakes to be about 5 inches in across – these can be rolled to keep warm while removing the other pancakes. Best to serve warm, but don't be surprised if someone opens the refrigerator and eats a couple cold ones you thought you'd save for another meal. ☺

35 ~ JIM'S PRIZE-WINNING "DEEP DARK SECRET"

Both Jim's mother and his Aunt Alice made this dessert for Christmas Eve fairly regularly, so when Jim's church pitted the men against each other for a cake bake-off, he made this recipe. It won the taste test year-after-year so finally the judges insisted he enter a different recipe. The beautiful Christmas dessert can serve up to 20, so adjust it accordingly.

CRUST: Mix well: 4 eggs, well beaten; 1 cup flour, 1 and ½ cup sugar, ¼ teaspoon salt, 2 teaspoons baking powder (NOT SODA), 1 cup chopped dates, 1 cup chopped nuts of choice, and 2 teaspoons vanilla.

Spread out on a greased or parchment papered cookie sheet and let it bake for 30-45 minutes – browned lightly. When it's cool, break it into small pieces. Put ½ the pieces on the serving plate and gently heap onto the "crust," sliced fruits such as: bananas, cherries, oranges, grapes of various colors, and other soft fruits you enjoy.

Lay the other broken cake pieces over and around the fruit. Carefully pour the contents of one medium can of crushed pineapple on top of the cake pieces.

Top the dessert with thick whipped topping, such as Coolwhip. Drain maraschino cherries and use as garnish along with pecan halves. Let it stand in the refrigerator for at least an hour before serving.

36 ~ OSTKAKA (A SWEDISH DESSERT)

2 qt. whole milk
½ cup flour
½ c milk
½ rennet tablet
2 eggs

½ cup sugar
1 cup light or half/half cream
½ tsp. salt
1 tsp. almond extract

Heat milk to barely lukewarm. Mix flour into ½ cup milk and mix until smooth; add to the lukewarm milk and mix well. Dissolve the rennet in 1 tablespoon of lukewarm water and mix into the milk. Let set for 10 minutes until set. Do not stir. Cut the curd and let set a few minutes until it separates. Drain off the whey gradually. Beat eggs and mix sugar, salt, and extract with 1 cup light cream into the curd. Pour into well greased pan and bake at 300 degrees for 1 and a half hours, but turn up the heat at the end to lightly brown the top. It's done with it's firm. Serve warm or cold with lingonberries or other sweet berries and top with whipped cream.

37 ~ SWEDISH RICE PUDDING

JUDY KISBY

1 c. uncooked rice
1 ½ tsp. lemon
¾ tsp. cardamom
Raisins (optional)

6 separated eggs

6 c. milk
4½ Tbsp. cornstarch
Pinch of salt
¾ c. sugar

Cook rice according to package. Scald 4 cups of milk. Add rice. Mix sugar, cornstarch, and salt. Add 2 cups cold milk. Add to hot mixture. Cook 20 minutes. Gradually add slightly beaten egg yolks and cardamom. Cook a couple of minutes. Pour into baking dish. Cover with meringue made with 6 egg whites and 12 tablespoons sugar. Brown in oven. Can be served with the main course instead of potatoes, but it also can be a dessert.

38 ~ CHRISTMAS STARS

MARGERY KISBY WARDER

1 c butter	½ c brown sugar	2 ½ c white flour

Cream together: 1 cup butter and one-half cup brown sugar. Gradually add 2 and one-half cups of regular white flour. Chill for about an hour. Roll out with a rolling pin to about 1/3 inch thickness and use star cookie cutter to make stars you can bake for about 20-25 minutes at a LOW temperature of 250 degrees. If desired, you can frost these, but you won't feel quite as guilty eating this slightly less sweet cookie if you just enjoy it with friends as is.

39 ~ CHRISTMAS SNOWBALLS

There are lots of variations on this recipe. You can call them Russian teacakes, Mexican wedding cakes, pecan this or that, and you can call them Christmas snowballs – but most cookie exchanges like to have someone bring these round powdered sugar treats. You can vary how the finished cookie looks if you want variety and are short on time. Roll the cookie in powdered or white or colored sugars when warm, or dip in a chocolate or other frosting, adding candy sprinkles. OR wrap the dough around a chocolate candy "kiss" or a pecan half. Some drizzle chocolate or caramel over the baked cookie. This cookie sets your creativity free! Regardless, have on hand: room temperature butter, powdered sugar, flour, salt, vanilla, and your favorite nuts.

Start the mixer fairly low and gradually add these ingredients so they are "creamed" together:

1 cup room temperature butter	one-half cup POWDERED sugar
2 and one fourth cup white flour	one eighth teaspoon salt
1 teaspoon vanilla	up to one cup chopped nuts

(I like using pecan pieces, not halves). Chill for about 30 minutes or until you can more easily roll into balls about one inch in diameter. Place on a good cookie sheet and bake at 300 degrees until a slight color change to very light brown. Roll the baked cookie in powdered sugar (or decorate as you desire) and let cool before storing or serving.

Devotionals

But as for me, the nearness of God is my good;

I have made the Lord my refuge, that I may

tell of your works.

Psalm 73:28 (N.A.S.B.)

40 ~ CHRISTMAS IS COMING

ARNOLD KROPP

"Yippee," the kiddies ponder, "what will Dad get me this year?"

Sadly, in this secular world, receiving gifts seems to be the most important part of the season we call Christmas, that next holiday a month after Thanksgiving. The malls are filled with people searching for that perfect gift. The stores have been stocked full of those beloved items to decorate the home—the lights and ornaments on the strategically placed fake tree, the lights decorating the outside and possibly a display of a manger scene. Hallmark has the latest in cards to send to relatives and friends near and far, or we can post a note on social media.

For most of the retail trade, their profits are determined by our gift shopping, so swipe the debit card until it hurts. We spend that cash we've been saving or we go into debt hoping to be able to pay it back before the Easter bunny appears. The day is so important that the stores start displaying the related items four months before that date recorded in history books as THE special day to celebrate as Christmas.

Oh, how our human nature interferes with the real meaning of our holiday celebrations. Now schools, lawyers and judges have deemed any mention of the meaning of Christmas as offensive and stores comply with greetings of "Happy Xmas."

Enough of that.

There is the holy, magnificent, one-and-only God, the Creator of this universe, the wonders of nature, (the vegetation we consume, tomatoes, watermelons and yams, the Creator of rose buds and poinsettias), the Creator of the animals, (butterflies and eagles, giraffes, ants and alligators). Then happens the creation of those first two humans made in His image with a physical body and spiritual soul.

After thousands of years of conflict and wars and rumors of war among us, God found a righteous man named Noah to start a new family of man. God positioned a rainbow to remind us to love one another, to follow those few commandments, and if we do that, all will be well.

But the conflicts, wars, and rumors of war continued.

So, God determined that enough is enough, and a new plan was initiated.

The Mighty One found a worthy young lady, a virgin, to give birth to His only Son; sending to us the Divine in a human body to live among us, to be one of us, to teach and share the heart of the Father God with us in our language so we could hear with our ears and see this Blessed One with our eyes so we'd understand and hopefully embrace Him.

Christmas is that selected time we celebrate in remembrance of the birth of the Savior Jesus bearing the sins of our waywardness.

PRAYER:

Father God, at times we, Your children here in this country, feel so helpless about the attacks upon us, evident in the waywardness the secular culture is taking us. We are fighting those who have left the way of righteousness to walk in darkness. It seems they rejoice in the evil they do. Help us as YOUR church to remain united. Help us to remain focused on Your graciousness, on Your forgiveness and lean not unto our own understandings, but to trust Your Word, to continue to acknowledge You, our God, in all we do, in all the ways we run our daily lives.

Let our happiness in knowing You be a testimony to those who have not believed and accepted Your forgiveness. We pray for our leaders in all positions, that they would cry out for knowledge, lifting their voices for understanding, seeking it as silver and as hidden treasure, and then boldly acknowledge the truth of Your Word. Your blessings have been upon this country from the beginning. In You they trusted, and now Lord God, we need discretion to preserve us and we need understanding to keep us united as one body, as members of the body of Christ our Lord.

Thank You Father, and now in the name of Jesus, we will stand united, we will let our light shine. Amen.

41 ~ WHAT TRUSTING GOD MEANS TO ME

CARLA (OLSON) RYDBERG

"Surely God is my salvation; I will trust and not be afraid. The Lord, the Lord Himself, is my strength and my defense; He has become my salvation"(Isaiah 12:2, NIV).

All I am and have first came from God – is there anything He could possibly desire? Realizing it always pleases God when I freely give Him my love and worship, I feel the special gift I can give God this year is my continued TRUST.

Trust His love for me even when fervent prayers are not answered as I would have wanted. Not a pain is felt or a grief pierces the soul but the throb vibrates to the Father's heart.

Rely on God as my strength and refuge even when it feels like God has removed His protective hand. Though our feelings come and go, God's love for us is constant.

Understand that I may not receive the answers to all the questions on my heart until the mysteries of heaven are revealed, but I can have confidence that God knows the end from the beginning. There should be no fear in trusting an unknown future to an all-knowing God.

Savor more time in prayer and God's Word to seek His desire for my life and allow Him to form in me a servant's heart.

Trust the truth of God's Word that promises, *"I know the plans I have for you,"* declares the Lord, *"plans to prosper you and not to harm you, plans to give you a hope and a future"* (Jeremiah 29:11, NIV).

I know there will be days when I waiver in giving God my gift of trust, so I'm thankful that His mercies are new every morning. God's compassion and understanding are deeper and wider than we can ever comprehend and His faithfulness reaches to the skies.

PRAYER:

Holy Lord, My life is in Your hands. Thank You for filling my heart with steadfast hope and peace that passes understanding as I place my trust in You. Amen.

42 ~ WHAT CAN I GIVE HIM?

KAREN MEAD

What can I give Him? I need to give Him what I value the most, and that is time! It seems to be in such short supply. God has given me the gift of time on Earth. Jesus' gift is eternal life and time will no longer be a factor. Hallelujah!!

While on Earth, I need to give my time to God in praise and thanksgiving.

Psalm 34:1 says, *"I will bless the Lord at all times; His praise shall continually be in my mouth"* *(NASB)*.

Ephesians 5:20 says, *"Always giving thanks to God the Father for everything, in the name of our Lord Jesus Christ"* *(NIV)*. In order to develop friendship with God, I need to give Him my time and energy. What better way could I spend my time?

I need to give my time to God by serving others. I must value what God values. I must care about the people that God cares about. Ephesians 5:15-16 says, *"Therefore be careful how you walk, not as unwise men, but as wise, making the most of your time, because the days are evil"* *(NASB)*. Whether in the church, on my job, or in the community, there are always people that need time. It might be a physical need, or they might just need someone to talk to.

PRAYER:

Dear Jesus, Thank You for coming to Earth to live among us and for dying for our sins so that we can live with You forever. Help me, Lord, to use my time everyday loving and serving You. Amen

43 ~ HERE I AM, LORD

GEORGIA CLARK

"Then I the Lord asking, 'Whom shall I send....Who will go?'
and I said, 'Here am I! Send me.'" (Isaiah 6:8, NIV)

What could I give Him? How often do I think of giving Jesus something? It's almost always, "Dear Jesus, please give me this or do that," if, in all the hustle of gift-giving to everyone else, I even think of a gift for Him.

God gave me and you all we needed when He sent Jesus. After His birth, we've always read that the wise men came to visit the baby, bearing gifts. Despite hearing and knowing that beautiful story for years, I'm not sure I've ever really dwelt on what **I** can give **Him** as a gift.

Of course I know I'm to give Him my heart, as I did years ago as a child. God then convinced me, years later, that I needed to be fully His and recognize Him not only as Savior but also as Lord. And I know this is truly all that's important and what He most wants.

But "What (gift) could **I** give **Him**?"

Years ago, a wise Christian lady told me, as I was searching for an answer as to whether I should serve in a specific Christian position, "God doesn't want your **ability** as much as He wants your **availability**."

I've never forgotten those words. Despite the fact that it may not be scriptural, I do believe that God just wants me to be available, not just for what I like to do, but for any task He has for me.

PRAYER:

Father, thank You for the wondrous gift of Your Son. Thank You for stirring my heart to give back to You. Help me to always be ready to say, when it's Your will, "Here I am, send me." Amen.

44 ~ THE GIFT OF TIME

HAROLD CLARK

There is a right time for everything:
A time to be born, A time to die;
A time to plant; A time to harvest;
A time to kill; A time to heal;
A time to destroy: A time to rebuild;
A time to cry; A time to laugh;
A time to grieve; A time to dance;
A time to hug; A time not to hug;
A time for keeping; A time for throwing away;
A time to tear; A time to repair;
A time to be quiet; A time to speak up;
A time for loving; A time for hating;
A time for war; A time for peace." (Ecclesiastes 3:1-8 TLB)

What can I give Jesus? I can give Him my time.

If you really knew me well, you'd know that one of the things I have that I guard closely and don't give away easily is my time. It's no problem for me to be more selfish with it than with my money. To me, time is more valuable than wealth.

Because of this, I know I **need to** and even have come to **want to** give God my time. He has blessed me with willingness to share my time for Him.

Time is what I can give:
Time to do daily devotions, time to study the Word;
Time to pray, time to help others;
Time to serve the Lord, time to join others in worship;
Time to give thanks for God's saving grace.
Time to enjoy my children and grandchild, and
Time to enjoy the outdoors.

PRAYER:
Lord, help me use Your time wisely. Help me not be selfish with the time You have given me and help me to give it willingly and joyfully. Amen.

45 ~ CLOSE ENOUGH

BARBARA GORDON

"Come near to God and He will come near to you." (James 4:8a NIV)

Really? Not again.

The manger scene on the box appears so serene. Apparently *serene* is not the sought after look of our youngest son, Alex. Every time he saunters past the display, he scoots the characters toward center stage. As she cradles her baby, Mary stands close enough to kiss Joseph. The shepherds and wise men hold hands as the animals huddle under their feet. Shaking my head, I correct the disarray on my next trip through the family room. My family claims they can tell who walked through the family room last by the placement of the Holy Family.

On Christmas Eve, the crystal lights on our tree winked in synchronization. While the fruit and spices simmered, fragrance filled the room. A rare December snow swirled outside, casting a halo around the streetlights. Perfection.

I softly hummed "Away in a Manger." With arms loaded with paper, ribbon and tape, I headed for the bedroom to wrap those last few presents. I froze in my steps when I heard Alex's whispered utterance.

"They can't see the baby Jesus."

The words were Alex's; the fluttering in my soul was the Spirit. Maybe, just maybe, the picture on the box was wrong after all.

My prayer, this holiday season and always, is that we come near enough to see Jesus.

PRAYER:
Precious Father, help us confirm that your Son, the world's Savior, is the center of our Christmas celebration. Amen.

46 ~ JUST A FANCY, BUT EMPTY, BOX

PAUL WARDER

My wife Margery and I went to a church Christmas concert. There were Christmas lights and decorated trees, but the most meaningful part to me was the words of the songs sung by the choir and played by the orchestra. The words and music proclaimed not just the birth of a baby, but also the birth of Him as the Savior, the Messiah, the Christ. The words were meaningful because some of them spoke not just of the birth of a baby, though a special baby, but the birth of One who would live a sinless life, pay for our sins by dying on a cross, and give us hope forever by His resurrection from the dead. That acknowledgement of Jesus as the Savior, Messiah, the Christ, was why the songs were memorable, and why even the decorations had meaning.

As I sat at that concert, I began to think: "How do people celebrate Christmas without having faith in Christ? More importantly, *why* do they celebrate Christmas at all, if they do not want anything to do with Him the rest of the year? Oh, probably many people who do not want anything to do with Jesus will put up lights and decorations outside, send out Christmas cards, put up a Christmas tree, exchange presents with friends and loved ones, host and go to parties, and gather on December 25 with family.

What an odd thing to celebrate *Christ*mas without *Christ*! As some writers have suggested many times, to celebrate Christmas without Christ is like having a birthday party where the person having the birthday is excluded.

However, as I sat at that concert, I thought of a different image. It's the image of some boxes we have on the shelves in our utility room. Among other things, these shelves hold Christmas wrapping paper, unused Christmas cards for the next year, some brackets to hang lights on the gutters, and some fancy, but empty, boxes. These boxes are colorful, some even have ribbon, but they are empty until someone puts a gift inside. This is the image I have of celebrating Christmas without Christ. We may have all the outward colorful trappings and the hustle and bustle of the season, but the end result is a hollow shell, an empty box lacking "the reason for the season."

One other thing. There are people and stores who say we should not say, "Merry Christmas" anymore because it might offend those who do not believe in Christ. I would say that for those who do not believe in Christ, please do not worry about putting up lights, sending out cards, and exchanging gifts. In fact, if "Merry Christmas" is so offensive, then maybe that person should go to work as usual on December 25.

Better instead, look seriously into the Christ of Christmas. Discover Him for yourself. Ask Him to forgive your sin and come into your life to be the Lord of your life. Truly celebrate *Christ*mas by celebrating *His* birth, *His* death, and *His* resurrection so that all the lights and cards and presents and gatherings are something more than just a fancy, but empty, box.

"But mark this: there will be terrible times in the last days. People will be… having a form of godliness but denying its power…" (2 Timothy 3:1,2a, 5a NIV)

"You hypocrites, rightly did Isaiah prophesy of you: 'This people honors me with their lips, but their heart is far away from Me.'" (Matthew 15:7, 8 NASB)

(A POSSIBLE PRAYER YOU MIGHT SAY:)

Lord Jesus, I know I can be easily distracted by the outward display of Christmas—the programs, the gatherings, the gift buying and giving, and even the decorating of my house. Help me, Lord, instead, to make You the center of Christmas, the focus of Christmas, the main purpose of Christmas. May I honor You not only with my words, but also with my actions and my intentions, as not only the Babe in a manger, but as MY crucified and risen Savior. Thank You for coming to earth for us. Amen.

47 ~ WE SINNERS NEED A SAVIOR

MARGERY KISBY WARDER

"Unto you is born this day...a Savior, who is Christ the Lord" (Luke 2:11 RSV).

"You shall call His name Jesus, for He will save His people from their sins" (Matthew 1:21 RSV).

When I think about Baby Jesus in the manger, I am reminded that He came to us because our sins separated us from God. God's love wanted the "sin barrier" removed. God loves us like we are, but He sent His Son so we could be forgiven and become incresingly Christ-like. Unless we invited Jesus to become our Savior, we will have to spend eternity paying for our sins ourselves. How foolish to do that when God sent us eternal life as His gift to those who trust, who believe in His Son.

Because God is holy, He cannot be in the presence of sin. Sin makes God turn His face away. Remember the definition of sin? Sin is everything in word, thought, or deed that is contrary to the perfect will of God. In the book of James, chapter 4, verse 17, we read, *"Whoever knows what is right to do and fails to do it, for him it is a sin" (RSV).* We'd all probably agree with the Bible, in 1st John 1:8-9 when it says that we have sinned.

Why does God take sin so seriously? Our sin mimics our first parents' sin. When we sin, we question God's authority; we challenge His wisdom and judgment; we substitute our own opinion for God's. Basically, we distrust God's goodness because we think we know best about what is right for us. When we pridefully act contrary to God's Word, in essence we doubt His integrity and truthfulness.

If I excuse my sin, treating it as, "this one doesn't matter," I'm trying to bypass God's system of justice or I'm willfully imposing upon God's mercy and grace, as if I had the right to snatch those gifts of grace and mercy from God's hand. God hates sin because sin keeps me from the fellowship God desires to have with me.

When I rethink how abhorrent my sin is to God, I admit I need Someone to save me from the consequences of my sin – I need a Savior! I am so thankful God loved us/me enough to send His sinless, perfect Son to take the punishment our/my sin deserved. The news that God sent us One who will become our Savior if we sincerely ask Him to – Oh, my! That is indeed good news! One of Jesus' closest followers wrote, *"But to all who received Him/Jesus, who believed in His name, He gave power to become children of God, who were born not of blood nor of the will of the flesh, nor of the will of man, but of God" (John 1:12-13, RSV).*

PRAYER:

Thank you Father God, for loving us before we deserved to be loved, with a love that would send Your Son to take the punishment for our sins. I repent of my sinfulness. Thank you, Jesus, for purchasing our redemption and leaving the Holy Spirit to live within all who trust You as Savior. May I live like one changed by You until I am in Your presence. In Jesus' name, Amen.

Brain Teasers

For the Lord gives wisdom; from His mouth come knowledge and understanding.

Proverbs 2:6 (NASB)

48 ~ABC'S OF FAMILY CHRISTMAS MINISTRIES

JANE LANDRETH

Use these activities to help you or your family minister to others during the Christmas holidays. Check each activity off when it has been completed.

_____ A Attend a Christmas service.

_____ B Bake bread and give to an elderly neighbor.

_____ C Go Christmas caroling.

_____ D Deliver Christmas baskets to the needy.

_____ E Entertain a family that attends your church.

_____ F Surprise someone with a fruit basket.

_____ G Give canned goods to the church food pantry.

_____ H Share holiday greeting cards with friends.

_____ I Invite someone to share a meal with your family.

_____ J Join in with others to sing the Christmas hymns at church.

_____ K Keep Christ in Christmas by sharing the Bible's Christmas story.

_____ L Write a letter to someone living away.

_____ M Make cookies and take to a friend.

_____ N Think of the many names of Jesus and share with someone.

_____ O Offer to do shopping for a senior adult.

_____ P Pray for someone who needs to hear about Jesus.

_____ Q Spend quality time together with family or friends.

_____ R Read the Christmas story from the Bible—Luke 2.

_____ S Sing praises and worship God.

_____ T Take a Christmas surprise to someone lonely.

_____ U Unite with a friend and tell why God sent His Son Jesus.

_____ V Visit a nursing home.

_____ W Wrap a gift for someone from the Christmas tree ministry.

_____ X Share your eXcitement of Christmas with someone.

_____ Y Yell, "Merry Christmas!" to someone in the neighborhood.

_____ Z Zealously tell someone about Jesus' birth.

When completed, thank God for helping you or your family to minister to others during this Christmas season!

49 ~ CHRISTMAS ABC'S BIBLE QUIZ

JANE LANDRETH

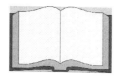

Knowing the Christmas Bible story is important. Fill in the blanks of these ABC Christmas statements by looking up the Bible verse in the Revised Standard Version Bible. (If you don't have that version in your home, you can use it by going to **https://www.biblegateway.com** and selecting "Revised Standard Version" in the search box provided.)

A _____ waited for the coming Messiah. Luke 2:36.

B Mary gave _____ to her first-born son. Luke 2:7.

C The child will be wrapped in _____. Luke 2:12.

D Jesus descended from the family of _____. Luke 2:4.

E Wise men came from the _____ to see Jesus. Matthew 2:1.

F The shepherds kept watch over their _____. Luke 2:8.

G The Wise Men brought Jesus some _____. Matthew 2:11.

H The angels say, "Glory to God in the _____." Luke 2:14.

I Joseph and Mary found no room in the _____. Luke 2:7.

J The baby was to be named _____. Matthew 1:21.

K Herod was the _____ at this time. Matthew 2:1.

L After the angels left, the shepherds said, "_____ us go to Bethlehem." Luke 2:15.

M Mary placed the baby in a _____. Luke 2:7.

N Mary and Joseph found _____ room in the inn. Luke 2:7.

O The Wise Men _____ their treasures for Jesus. Matthew 2:11.

P Mary _____ all the events in her heart. Matthew 2:19.

Q Census was taken when _____ was governor of Syria. Luke 2:2.

R After seeing the baby, the shepherds _____ to the fields glorifying and praising God. Luke 2:20.

S King Herod told the Wise Men to _____ for the baby. Matthew 2:8.

T The _____ came for Mary to have the baby. Luke 2:7.

U The angel said to Mary, "The Holy Spirit will come _____ you." Luke 1:35.

V A _____ named Mary will bear the son, Jesus. Luke 1:27.

W The _____ Men followed the star. Matthew 2:1,2.

X Mary was much _ _ _ _ _ _ x _ _ by Gabriel's words. Luke 1:28.

Y "I bring _____ tidings of great joy," said the angel. Luke 2:10.

Z _ _ z _ _ _ _ _ , the town Mary and Joseph were from. Luke 2:4.

116

50 ~ THEY SHALL CALL HIS NAME JESUS

JANE LANDRETH

Do you know how you got your name? Why was your name given to you? Who named you?

My mother named me for my doctor, Mary. My grandmother's middle name was Jane. So my mother called me, Mary Jane. Much to her surprise, the doctor's name was really Mary Jane.

Many names have special meanings. For example: David means "much loved"; Ruth means "friendship"; Nathan means "gift"; Sarah means "princess."

Mary and Joseph knew before God's Son was born what He would be named. An angel had appeared to them and told each of them to call His name, JESUS, which means Savior.

The Bible tells us many other names or descriptions of Jesus. Unscramble the words below to discover some of those names.

lEemumna _____   raTheec _____

rhitsC _____   heerSpdh _____

sieMsha _____   odrL _____

rePcni fo Pacee _____   ____ _____

fluWdreno isnuCureo _____   _____

onS fo odG _____ ___ _____   ignK _____

A: Emmanuel, Teacher, Christ, Shepherd, Messiah, Lord, Prince of Peace, Wonderful Counselor, Son of God, King.

Christmas Crossword Puzzle

Use Matthew 1 & 2 and Luke 1 & 2 for clues

~ 51 ~

ACROSS
4 Number of Gospels
5 Name of Mary's cousin
7 Record of promise
8 Month Gabriel visited Nazareth
9 Number of kinds of gifts
10 God-with-us
12 Asked, "Where is He that is
born King of the Jews?"
14 Priest visited by angel
15 Mary declared herself to be this

DOWN
1 Visited Mary, Joseph, shepherds
2 Stepfather/Guardian of Jesus
3 First "missionaries"
6 Mary's question to angel
11 Name angel told Joseph to call
Mary's child when He was born
13 Where Zacharias wrote his son's
name to settle an argument

"Puzzle made at puzzle-maker.com" by Margery Warder

*Answers: Across -Four, Elizabeth, prophecy, sixth, three, Emmanuel,
Wisemen, Zacharias, Handmaid of the Lord
Down: Angels, Joseph, shepherds, How can this be, Gabriel, Jesus,
tablet*

52 ~ CHRISTMAS WORD FIND

```
H A N D M A I D E N O F T H E L O R D
W W A N G E L S P D Y Y S D P Y L R B
Y B I P Y J M B T Q S D R L P P M Y B
S 1 3 S I S E N E G R O T E L B A T S
D J D X E Y L P T E Q D N P G R V Y V
P I Z W L M X G H V Y J X O Y N K N N
Z B V N B B E P H J Z X W R F G A Q M
V J M A L T E N T T H D J J Q G E M M
T W J P D H X K L E E Z M D K N O T G
H B Q M S Z Z L R B T R D G R N J D N
G P T Q R N Y O P W E Z A N N E R W Q
Y J E Q G N D G T P M T J Z R J N V V
T B P S Y M L K E K B T H U A X L J N
Z L R Q O R G E Y T M G S L T N B T N
Y Q N T D J K G W K Y A N N E R J V M
N W D B Y N N N Y D L V Y G R H D D L
Y Z T D N Y V M N E J T L L R W E Q Y
P M N I L R N Z M G M P L B T D N M J
```

City of David/ancestral home of Joseph and Mary – Be____

Hometown of Joseph – N_____

Stepfather of Jesus – J_____

Mary called herself this – H_____ __ _____ _L____

Holy Family fled to -- E_____

Jealous king in Jerusalem - _____

Where wisemen asked for directions – J__

Travelers who brought gifts – W____

Where Mary laid the Son of God – M___

Proclaimers of Glory – A____

Startled sheep-watchers – S____

First prophecy about Jesus – G____

Kingly ancestral line – D__

Jesus came as the –S__ of G____

Shelter for the night – I__

Man eager for a "do over" – I_____

ANSWERS TO CHRISTMAS WORD FIND

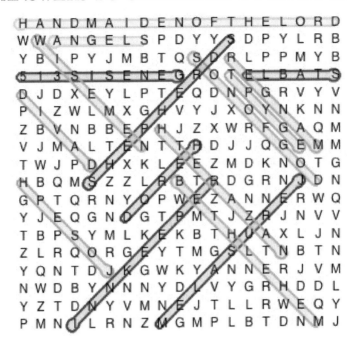

"Puzzle made at puzzle-maker.com"
Word Find created on Puzzlemaker.com by Margery Kisby Warder

Fiction

"...whatever is true, whatever is honorable, whatever is just, whatever is pure, whatever is lovely, whatever is gracious, if there be any excellence, if there is anything worthy of praise, think about these things."
(Philippians 4:8 RSV)

53 ~ THE WATCHER'S GIFT

SANDY JORDAN

Mary stood behind the buffalo-hide curtain waiting for the Bird City Christmas Pageant to begin. She fought the desire to dash out into the night, away from the townspeople gathered in the old log schoolhouse. She couldn't leave. She'd made a promise, and promises had to be kept, regardless of the cost. Tonight humility would extract a high price from her. Tonight she would have to pick up the old, dilapidated, battered fiddle that sat on a nearby chair and play it in front of everyone. She shuddered at the thought of the raspy voice she would endure while she played a few notes to fulfill her obligation. Maybe if she'd never known more . . .

Closing her eyes, Mary could see the music room of her old home in Three Pines, Georgia. One by one, she pictured her musically gifted family. Papa made music seem as natural as breathing and proved it with his booming bass voice and fiddle. Mamma's fingers plucked the harp with precision as her high lilting soprano voice matched the smiles she bestowed upon their children. Her sister Beth played the piano and Mary's brothers sang along.

Mary's earliest memories were climbing up onto the piano bench and pecking at the keys until the song sounded right. At five, when no one was around, she managed to pull Papa's fiddle down and began teaching herself to play. By her seventh birthday, her family encouraged Mary to begin playing along as they filled their home with music. Her fear about not matching their skill was met with protests and assurances of how much they hoped she could finally join them. What delightful times those had been. Each night, after Mamma turned out the lamps, Mary lay in her bed hoping nothing would ever disrupt the harmony that lingered long after the last chords had grown silent.

Then came the War Between the States. Music faded. Papa and her brothers put their boots in stirrups, waved farewell, and rode away to fight at places called Bull Run and Shiloh. Papa came home to rest in the graveyard first, and then Aaron, her oldest brother. Life without the men to provide became more challenging. The majority of the servants left. Just last February, Beth had gone to visit a cousin and died of the scarlet fever. Laying her beside Papa, Mamma had grown silent.

When a sympathetic letter from Mamma's brother suggested a change might do them good, Mamma's countenance changed ever so slightly. With little forethought or preparation, they left behind the monuments to their sorrow and travelled with their old loyal servant Juba and his son until they reached Bird City, Kansas. It was a change, but not a paradise. Now they lived with Uncle Josh in a small cabin near the old log school and church.

Mamma was in Kansas but her broken heart longed for the happiness of her past. Mary took on most of the housekeeping and cooking responsibilities. Though it seemed an overwhelming task for a child of eleven, Mary pushed and pulled and shoved their scant belongings to mix in with Uncle Josh's, hoping to make the log cabin more pleasant. When Mamma or Uncle Josh encouraged her to not work so hard, she wandered along the dusty streets of their small community.

One forenoon, Mary's walk brought her across a discarded wooden box behind the school. Weathered planks, perhaps set aside by volunteers who rebuilt the school's small stage last summer, leaned protectively against the box. Obviously the last curious person who rummaged through the box hadn't bothered to tuck in all its contents. Disheveled sun-bleached fabric spilled over the edge. Mary felt compelled to investigate; perhaps there would be something salvageable Mamma would appreciate.

Moving the boards enough to open the box, Mary wasn't sure how to appraise the odds and ends. Her hands lifted and sorted through a frayed oval rug, a hammer's broken handle, half of a ceramic pitcher someone must have once prized, perhaps before a rough journey in a covered wagon, and a threadbare quilt. Nothing useful. Who knew if some critter claimed the quilt a perfect home? Mary didn't want to mess with critters. She was about to close the lid when her eyes spied a scroll and pegbox poking out through a tear in the quilt.

Could it be? It had to be a fiddle! She felt a rush of excitement. Imagine, music! Her fingers tugged gently at the quilt, not wanting to damage a fragile instrument. With each tug, her hopes vanished. She picked up the dilapidated, unkempt fiddle in her hands, turning it over and shaking it in case the fiddle's body had rodent residents. She set it aside and dug through the box. The bow was still intact, but how impossible it would be to make that fiddle sing. Why hadn't the previous owner at least kept it inside the case? Ah, maybe he'd tried. The case was there, too, but watermarks told part of its history. No wonder it no longer closed properly and no wonder the fasteners were useless.

Out of concern for Mamma's fragile heart, Mary kept her discovery a secret and stowed the fiddle away in a safe place. Often, though, Mary carried the case with her to a secluded place just outside of town. She loosened and tightened the strings, hoping the cracked bridge would hold together for another song. She experimented, trying to convince the abused instrument it was crafted to sing.

Early one morning as Mary coaxed the fiddle's strings to make peace with a tune, Mary became aware of The Watcher, a tall man, gaunt with long white hair and beard. He wore the fringed buckskin of the frontier. From a distance, he studied as her hand slid the bow first one way, then another, across the fiddle. He listened and nodded, but he never moved closer or bothered her.

After that, Mary told Mamma about the old fiddle she'd found. When Mamma saw it, she suggested Mary take it out to the woodpile. Since it wasn't an order, Mary saw no harm in keeping the fiddle, but when she fought the fiddle for music, she did so on the far side of the school so Mamma wouldn't have to hear it.

The Watcher wasn't the only one who happened upon Mary as she played the fiddle. When Miss Adams, her teacher, came to school earlier than usual to start the fire and prepare the classroom, she found Mary playing the fiddle. Before she could finish her comment about Mary's playing, Mary, embarrassed, threw down the fiddle and ran from the school into the tall prairie grasses.

Mary's strength failed her as she fought her way through the tall grass. She felt helpless. Frustrated that her carelessness had permitted others to hear her screeching sounds on the fiddle and worried that Mamma's sorrow might deepen when she realized how desperately her daughter longed for the way life had been before their move, Mary felt overwhelmed. Mamma needed Mary to be strong, but as Mary sank into the tall grasses, tears streamed down her cheeks. She didn't want to be taking care of her mother; she wanted Mamma taking care of her. "Oh, God," she prayed, "please make Mamma better so all our hearts can stop breaking." She curled up as tightly as she could and didn't mind when snowflakes began drifting down upon her.

Uncle Josh tracked his niece through the stomped down brown grasses now dusted with snow. He bent down and pulled her close. Speaking softly as sobs jerked her tired and sorrowing body, he told her how worried he'd been that she might get lost in the tall grass prairie. After a time, he said, "We better get up and go back into town, Mary. There's a puzzled schoolteacher who wonders why you were so rude. She wants to know you are safe. I think you need to apologize for running away from her when she called to you."

Miss Adams did want an explanation and an apology for Mary's disobedience. Why had she not come when her teacher had called to her? Mary knew Mamma did not need one more worry and Uncle Josh agreed that was sensible. They discussed how Mary could demonstrate genuine repentance if they kept her behavior between them without reporting it to her mother. That's when the bargain was reached. The teacher asked Mary to play the school's morning hymn on the fiddle and told her she also needed something more for the upcoming Christmas program. If Mary agreed to those conditions, Mamma would never need to learn of Mary's misconduct.

Now a cold wind wrapped around her ankles brought Mary's thoughts back to the schoolhouse. Even with woolen socks she felt the cold of the Kansas plains. She stepped up to the edge of the curtain and looked out. The school's Father Christmas moved among the crowd. Ah, she recognized him, though she had never learned his name. The Watcher's clothes still glistened with bits of melting snow as he held his big poke sack.

Helen, a small first grader, passed out gifts wrapped in brown paper to whichever recipient The Watcher indicated. Mary felt relieved to be mostly hidden behind the curtain. Her name wouldn't be on any gift because Christmas wasn't coming to any in their cabin this year. Now she and Mamma lived one day at a time; the old way of doing things was past.

The Watcher finished distributing gifts from his poke sack. He tucked it awkwardly under his arm and began walking toward the stage. Mary stepped back. Her heart pounded. She wanted no gift, nothing to stir the memories that hurt so bad.

The Watcher reached for the old fiddle, put it in its old case, closed the lid, and set it on the floor. Then he reached down for his poke sack and from it he lifted out something in a soft, tanned sheepskin, bulging and odd-shaped. He set it across the empty chair. "Open it, Mary. It's yours."

Confused, Mary's cold fingers fumbled with the leather fasteners on the fringed smooth case. She folded back the flap. Inside, resting snugly within the pressed down and slightly stained wool was a well-worn but perfect fiddle, glowing from use and tender care. She looked up at The Watcher.

"Play it Mary, play it for them and for me."

In his eyes she saw understanding and kindness. "Mary, your family will live in your music. It is not wrong to be happy." His gloved finger caught her tear.

Mary took the fiddle and bow and tucked it under her chin. Closing her eyes, she saw her family in their music room. She listened for the voices once so familiar. "Play for us, Mary," had not they urged her to play years ago when she'd held a fine instrument but she felt unworthy to join them? Eyes still closed, their encouraging faces of years before came into view, nodding, urging her to let her talent show so music could be shared as music was meant to be.

Stepping through the curtain's gap, Mary began playing "Silent Night," half expecting her family's harmony to fill the air. No, the voices were not the family's, but Mary listened as harsh voices of the Kansas settlers tried to blend their German and Swedish accents. Wait. Wait, could it be? Yes, now rising above and higher them all was her mamma's pure voice lilting from the back of the room to bless her daughter's Christmas offering.

Ah, that was hope. Yes, there was a new life for them in this frontier town of Bird City, Kansas. Mary felt joy welling up inside and she bid it escape through her music. She had dreaded the bargain that brought her to the stage, but now she wished the composers had written more verses to "Silent Night," for she would play them all.

The Watcher sat on the front row. Tears filled his gentle blue eyes. On his lap, Helen nestled under his beard. Mary played for The Watcher in the front row, for those gathered around him, and she played for loved ones resting in the tiny graveyard in Georgia, so far away...but so close in her heart on this Christmas night.

54 ~ THE NO KIDS CHRISTMAS PARTY

JANE LANDRETH

"What fun is a party without kids?" asked Madison. She and her twin brother were putting the last of their costumes into the bags.

"Doesn't sound like fun, but we promised Mom and Dad," said Jonathon. "Wish we didn't have to go, but they are counting on us to help entertain the people at the Heritage Nursing Home."

"Guess we better get going," said Madison picking up the bag. "The sooner we go, the sooner this party will be over."

"At least Dalton is looking forward to this evening. He has about worn out his costume by trying it on so many times," said Jonathon, picking up the staff Dad had made for him to use as a shepherd."

"All ready?" Mom asked as the children came into the living room.

"I am," shouted four-year-old Dalton who was jumping about the room excitedly.

"We can see that," said Madison. Her voice revealed a bit of the anger she felt at her brother's eagerness about the dull evening that awaited her.

"All set?" Dad's voice sounded from the next room. He came in carrying the manger he had built. It was filled with hay.

"Did you forget the doll we plan to use for baby Jesus?" asked Mom looking at Madison.

"I'll get it," Madison said as she hurried to her room. Soon she returned with the doll wrapped in a blanket.

"We'd better get started," said Dad. "A lot of people are waiting for us to give them a special Christmas visit. We don't want to keep them waiting too long."

"Sure wish there were going to be other kids at the party," Madison whispered to her twin as they hurried to the car.

"Me, too. It would be better than having a bunch of older people," grumbled Jonathon.

When they arrived at the Heritage Nursing Home, they saw a tall Christmas tree with bright decorations. It was standing near the entrance of the activity room where a group of men and women were gathered quietly.

When the family entered, several ladies looked up to see them. "Look, some folks have come to see us," one of the ladies said. A smile slowly spread across her face as she pointed to them. "And look at those cute children."

"They're the first children we have seen in a long time," said an elderly man in a wheelchair. He moved his chair a bit closer to get a good look at the children.

"I didn't know there were going to be three fine children here," said a crippled man holding a cane. "I thought the party was just for us."

Dad helped lead the singing of Christmas carols while Mom played the piano. Soon several of the men and women were singing along as they remembered the songs they had sung for so many years. A few of the people only listened with smiling faces.

"I want to hear the children sing by themselves," said one of the ladies who had been listening quietly to all that was happening.

The children looked at one another. "I guess we can try," said Madison, looking at Jonathon.

"Let me sing, 'Away in a Manger,'" said Dalton. He began to loudly sing his favorite Christmas song.

The men and women clapped and shouted, "Thank you!"

Then the children sang "Silent Night" together. The people wanted them to sing another and another.

Finally it was time for the reading of the Christmas story. The family got ready for the drama as the chaplain of the nursing home began reading the story. "So Joseph traveled to Bethlehem to register with Mary, who was expecting a child."

Dad and Mom, dressed as Mary and Joseph stood off to one side as the chaplain open her Bible to Luke 2 and read. "Soon it was time for the baby to be born. There was no room for them in the inn."

Mom entered the front of the room and sat beside the manger where the baby Jesus lay. Dad followed Mom and stood beside her and the Child. The chaplain continued the story.

When it came time in the story for the shepherds, Jonathon, dressed as a shepherd, moved toward the front of the room. Dalton, dressed as a sheep, followed.

"Baa, baa," Dalton said repeatedly as he moved on all fours like a sheep.

"I was a sheep when I was a little boy," said one of the men who was watching the scene.

"I was a shepherd," said another man. "I wish I could have had a shepherd's staff like that one. I just had a broom handle to carry."

"Shh!" whispered a lady sitting next to the men. "I want to hear the story."

"An angel appeared to the shepherds," said the chaplain.

Madison, who was dressed like an angel, suddenly spoke, "Don't be afraid. I bring you Good News. A Savior has been born in Bethlehem.

You can find Him wrapped in cloth and lying in a manger."

"Isn't she a pretty angel?" one of the ladies whispered to another.

Suddenly a loud chorus of praises began. "Glory to God in the highest, and on earth peace to men on whom His favor rests." All of the family had joined together to say what the angels in the Bible story had spoken.

"Let's go see Baby Jesus," said Jonathon.

Madison moved behind Mary and Joseph while Jonathon and the sheep moved toward the manger scene. Jonathon knelt down beside Baby Jesus.

They stayed in that scene as the chaplain finished telling the story.

When the story was over, the men and women clapped their hands. They thanked Madison, Jonathon, Dalton, and their parents for sharing the Christmas story with them.

"Before the refreshments, I have something to say," said Madison standing boldly in the front of the people. "I've learned the Christmas story doesn't end here."

Madison watched the people move closer in their chairs. Then she continued, "Jesus grew to be a child like us." She motioned to herself and her brothers. "Then Jesus grew to be a man who told others about God and did many miracles. But the greatest miracle of all was that God had sent Jesus to earth to be our Savior. Jesus died on the cross for our sins. Later He returned to heaven. If we have asked Jesus to forgive us and have accepted Him as our Savior, we will someday be in heaven with Him. So the Christmas story lives on."

"You have made this the best Christmas I have had in a long time," said one of the ladies with tears in her eyes.

"Oh, yes," agreed several of the people.

"Maybe you can come back and visit us again sometime," one lady said who had enjoyed seeing children.

"You can tell us some more Bible stories," said one of the men. "I like to hear stories about the Bible."

Jonathon looked at Madison and nodded. "Sure, we can do that."

"Baa, baa! I like it here!" yelled Dalton

The people at the Heritage Nursing Home laughed and clapped.

Dad told the people, "Perhaps we can bring several of the children's friends the next time we come since you like to see children."

Jonathon, Madison, and Dalton nodded and smiled.

On the way home, Jonathon remarked, "This 'No Other Kids' Party' turned out pretty good after all."

55 ~ AN UNEXPECTED CHRISTMAS

SUSAN HADDAN

Normally, I would be excited on Christmas Eve. I loved the experience of shopping for those special people in my life, decorating the tree, and the parties I absolutely lived for. It somehow didn't have the same feeling this year. But why? I couldn't put my finger on it. I had nearly everything I wanted. I'd long since decided against a "significant other" in my life. I was way too busy with work, my social life, and decorating my new home. My parents' marriage had ended in divorce and nearly everyone I talked to had the same misfortune in their family. Why would I want to set myself up for failure?

I don't know why I keep thinking about this, but yesterday when I was helping clean up after the office party, one of my coworkers, Kate, asked where I was going for Christmas. "Well, not to either of my parents' houses, that's for sure," I said. Actually, I wasn't sure what I was going to do. This guy, Drew, I had been seeing (and I think he's way more serious than I) had invited me to his apartment for drinks and a late Christmas dinner. After all, he is a great cook so how could I turn down a free meal? Kate told me I was more than welcome to celebrate Christmas with her and her family. I appreciated the invitation but I really didn't know Kate that well. Something kept gnawing at me inside telling me to accept the invitation.

I was picking out what I was going to wear to Drew's tomorrow and would you believe it - he called and cancelled! Seems his best friend from college is in town and they are making plans to go skiing in Colorado. Kate called fifteen minutes later wanting to know if I had changed my mind about coming. I didn't have anything better to do, so I accepted. I had no idea how we would come up with topics to talk about, but oh well. She has a couple little kids so maybe I can act silly with them and pass the day away.

I ultimately decided on a pair of new skinny jeans, boots, and a cute red sweater in honor of Christmas. Did I mention I love to buy new clothes? It's the absolute best way to pass a Saturday afternoon! I love picking out cute outfits for my little niece. I'm lucky to make the money I do. My sis is not so fortunate, so I'm glad I can help.

I popped some corn, opened a bottle of white wine, and curled up on the couch Christmas Eve and fully intended to watch a movie only to wake up after the movie had ended. I changed into my pajamas, brushed my teeth, and crawled into bed. Tomorrow was Christmas...What was so special about Christmas anyway?

I awoke on Christmas morning and looked out the window to see it had snowed. Not enough to hurt, just enough to make the outdoors look like a storybook fantasyland.

I dressed, grabbed a bottle of red wine from the cabinet for Kate and her husband and headed out the door. I was hoping the day would be a pleasant one full of conversation and maybe Kate and I could get to know each other better.

Kate's home was decorated beautifully and her kids were delightful. They were full of giggles and expectations of what was in all those lovely wrapped packages.

After making small talk, Kate turned to her husband, Wes, and asked that he read the Christmas story. I thought, "Hmm, you mean he's going to read an entire story before we eat?" The children quickly sat on either side of Kate and nestled next to her. Gee, it must be an exciting story. He opened a book that resembled the Bible and began reading, *"In those days, a decree went out...."*

I actually listened to the story, and it was interesting. I had never heard it before; this family was telling me that the birth of Jesus was what Christmas was all about. Don't get me wrong, Mom used to drop my sister and me off at Bible School in the summer so I have seen the inside of a church, but that's the size of it. I never considered it very important since my parents didn't seem interested. I guess I figured church was optional and just a social function of some sort. But today, in Kate's home, listening to a story of the birth of a baby boy named Jesus, stirred something inside me. What, I'm not sure.

We made small talk during dinner, which was delicious, by the way. Kate was a wonderful cook and seemed to love serving her family. After we had stuffed ourselves with cherry pie alamode, Wes took the girls into the family room while I helped Kate clear off the table.

I wished I could somehow get back on the subject of the story, but didn't know how to do that. I'm sure Kate would think I was really stupid knowing that's the first time I'd heard a story from the Bible. We cleared off the table in silence and got everything tucked away in the dishwasher. We were just about to walk into the family room when I noticed something on the wall that intrigued me. There, in an eight by ten inch frame, was a tea stained, worn doily, with a tattered page from a book. It was beautifully framed with lovely lace matting surrounding the items. I was curious about the story behind it.

I asked Kate what it was from. With tears in her eyes, she told me it had been her mother's. She had died suddenly two years ago in a car accident. Kate was going through her mother's things a few days after her death and came upon these verses in her Bible and they were underlined; Kate knew they must've been very special verses.

She decided then and there that her family should follow in those footsteps, too. The verses, she said, were found in Hebrews twelve, verses one and two, in the New American Standard Bible and it read as follows: *Therefore, since we have so great a cloud of witnesses surrounding us, let us also lay aside every encumbrance and the sin which so easily entangles us, and let us run with endurance the race that is set before us, fixing our eyes on Jesus, the author and perfecter of faith, who for the joy set before Him endured the cross, despising its shame, and has sat down at the right hand of the throne of God....*

I told Kate I was so sorry to bring up something that made her cry, especially on Christmas. She hugged me and told me it was quite alright. Kate asked me where I went to church, assuming I went somewhere. I embarrassingly told her I didn't attend church.

This was the moment I was looking for, so I took a deep breath and said, "Kate, you will probably be shocked at this, but I don't really know much, well, anything, about the Bible. I, well, we, never went to church growing up and my parents never seemed to put any importance on the Bible or church for that matter. And, to be honest, today when you all read that story in the Bible, well, it's the first time I've heard it and it intrigued me. Can you tell me more about this Jesus?"

Kate told me she had sensed an interest in me and had said a quick prayer asking for God's leading. Kate asked Wes to take the children out to play in the snow. He quickly bundled them up and whisked them out the door.

I told Kate she was lucky to have a husband who treated her like a princess. I'd never witnessed that kind of consideration between my mom and dad and that's why I never wanted to marry.

Kate told me Jesus was shining through Wes, that he'd become a Christian in college and his conversion had really changed his life.

I asked Kate if she was a Christian. She said she was. She had asked Jesus to be her Lord and Savior when she was ten years old. Kate told me about some of her experiences growing up and how the Lord had answered her prayers and that He was always there to help her, give her comfort, dissolve her fears, and guide her in her daily life.

"Gee," I thought, "this sounds too good to be true." Kate asked me if I would like to talk more about it or if I had questions. I said I did, so we got comfortable on the sofa and I asked a bunch of questions.

Kate got the Bible they'd read out earlier and started showing me several Bibles verses she comfortably explained along the way, like Romans 6:23 - *For the wages of sin is death but the gift of God is eternal life through Jesus Christ our Lord.*

Kate said we were all born out of sin and were as filthy rags but Jesus can cleanse us and make us white as snow; John 3:16 - *For God so loved the world that He gave His only begotten son that whosoever believeth in Him should not perish but have everlasting life.*

So, God sent His Son into a world full of sinners, to live among them and yet not sin even once. Then, Jesus was hung on a cross to die for all the sins of the world. He paid the price for my sins and the sins of everyone; Revelations 3:20 ~ *Behold I stand at the door and knock; if any man hear My voice and open the door, I will come in and sup with him and he with Me; 1 John 1:9 ~ If we confess our sins, He is faithful and just to forgive us our sins and to cleanse us from all unrighteousness.*

Kate told me that we must confess to God that we are sinners, ask forgiveness for our sins, believe on Him and we shall be saved and spend eternity in Heaven with our Lord and Savior.

I cannot explain how I felt at that moment, but I can tell you I've never wanted anything more in my life than salvation and to know Jesus as my personal Savior.

Kate led me in the sinner's prayer and right then, I felt a calm and total peace that I had never experienced. Kate gave me a Bible and a small guide so that I could acclimate myself to reading and studying.

Wes, Kate, the children and I spent the rest of the afternoon opening Christmas gifts. I enjoyed watching the kids play with their new toys and try on the new clothes they received. It was starting to get dark and I decided it was about time I headed home.

Kate walked me out to my car. I could feel myself tearing up as I looked at her. "Thank you for the Gift of today, Kate," I said. "This was the most precious Christmas I have ever experienced."

After all, she had introduced me to Jesus and I now have the best eternal home there could ever be.

Yesterday it had been just the usual Christmas, all about "stuff." Today? Well, today I have someone new in my heart—my Savior and Lord, Jesus Christ! Hallelujah!

56 ~ SHARING CHRISTMAS LOVE

JANE LANDRETH

"Mrs. Benson is watching us from her window," Tyler said, as he put a carrot nose on the snowman he and his sister were building.

"She looks sad," Allison said, looking toward the window. She straightened the snowman's mouth.

"Let's ask Mom why she is sad," said Tyler. They finished the snowman and went inside. Mom had hot chocolate and banana bread waiting for them.

Tyler and Allison sat down to enjoy their treat. Then Allison asked, "Mom, do you know why Mrs. Benson is sad?"

"Yes, I think I probably know. Mr. Benson passed away last summer," Mom said. "This will be her first Christmas without him."

"So she's all alone?" Allison asked. "Doesn't she have children?"

"Her daughter and grandchildren live far away," Mom explained. "Mrs. Benson told me they wouldn't be able to come have Christmas with her this year."

"That must be why she doesn't smile much," Tyler said. "Maybe we can help her have a happy Christmas."

"We could take her some of this banana bread I just made and visit with her later today," Mom suggested.

"Maybe a Christmas card would help," Tyler added. "We can each make one."

"Could we invite her to eat Christmas dinner with us?" Allison asked. "Grandma won't be able to be here this year. She is spending Christmas with Uncle Joe and Aunt Mary in Florida. Mrs. Benson could take her place."

"Those are all good ideas," Mom said. "Let's get busy."

Tyler got the crayons out of his room and Allison pulled some paper out of the desk. The children spent the afternoon making their Christmas cards for Mrs. Benson.

Later that afternoon, Mom and the children stepped onto the porch and rang Mrs. Benson's doorbell. In a few moments, the door opened.

"Surprise!" Tyler shouted. He handed Mrs. Benson his card. "I made you a picture of the snowman we made."

"I have one for you too," Allison said, handing her card to Mrs. Benson. "I made the manger scene because that is the real reason for Christmas."

"What a nice surprise," Mrs. Benson greeted them. "Come in, come in."

"We wanted to bring you some Christmas cheer," said Mom. She handed Mrs. Benson the loaf of banana bread. "Merry Christmas!"

"And we would like for you to have Christmas dinner with us," Allison added.

"We will be having Christmas with just our family this year," explained Mother. "We want you to join us."

"Oh, thank you!" Mrs. Benson's eyes were shiny with tears. "I'd like to have Christmas dinner with you. My family lives too far away to come for Christmas this year."

Then Tyler remembered. "We're going to read the Christmas story and have a birthday cake for Jesus on Christmas Eve. Maybe you would like to come celebrate Jesus' birth with us."

"Thank you for inviting me." Mrs. Benson smiled. "Of course, I'd enjoy celebrating Jesus' birthday with you."

As they left, Allison turned to wave to Mrs. Benson. "We'll see you on Christmas Eve," she called.

Mrs. Benson waved back. "Merry Christmas!" she said.

"Now Mrs. Benson won't be so lonely on Christmas," Allison said.

"She's smiling now too," added Tyler.

"You know, children," said Mom, "Jesus would be pleased with your idea of sharing Christmas love with Mrs. Benson.

57 ~ CHRISTMAS SOMETIMES HURTS
THOUGHTS AND A SHORT STORY

DOUG QUINN

"I wish we could just skip Christmas!"

"I dread the holidays. They're so hard. Especially Christmas!"

"Christmas was always her favorite time of the year; it will never again be the same."

Those sentiments and more are the desperate pleas resonating from the deep sorrow of those who grieve.

Not a year passes in our north-eastern Oklahoma community without about 1,000 citizens dying. Consequently, those who mourn loved ones are booked against their will for an unavoidable journey through a year of "Firsts." First wedding anniversary, first birthday, first Mother's Day, and ultimately, the arrival of the first Christmas without the presence of the beautiful person who was so much a part of life.

Christmas is often thought of as the most holy season. It's a time to celebrate generational traditions during a cherished reunion with family and treasured friends. But for one who has lost a loved one the previous year, life can feel so empty. The house echoes a new, foreign loneliness. One's mind longs for the presence of the one who died. While others are busily preparing for gatherings, the mourner wonders, "How can I ever get through the days ahead? How do I cope with this overwhelming loss during this special season?"

The loss of a significant person is a devastating event that imposes a change in our realities. We are forced to search for answers to new challenges; to find strength to endure a Christmas season in which others are experiencing joy, laughter, glad tidings, and fellowship.

The following short story lets us watch as Don deals with the loss of Sharon, the love of his life. I have entitled the story, "Christmas Hope."

CHRISTMAS HOPE

DOUG QUINN

The wind whipped around, stinging his cheek. The temperature had dropped all morning. Don hurried along the sidewalk in front of Brooks Food Palace. The arrival of October was bringing change, and not just in the weather. Just five months earlier Sharon reluctantly surrendered to cancer. A large seasonal display, "75 Shopping Days Until Christmas," surprised Don as he quickly entered the store to seek shelter from the cutting wind. The dreaded word *Christmas* momentarily stunned Don–a stark reminder the season he most feared alone was upon him. A new chill peppered him with goose bumps as deeply suppressed memories sprang forward!

Don had known all along this day would come, the first glaring reminder the Christmas season had arrived! He also knew he would have to find ways to "get through" this "*First* Christmas." But this would be much different! Mother's Day and the seventieth anniversary of Sharon's birthday had been tough, but as he sat those two out alone, interrupted only by a couple of thoughtful phone calls, he reminded himself those occasions only lasted 24 hours. Christmas lingered much longer, a "season" filled with day-after-day reminders of the countless ways Sharon absolutely loved the Christmas season. The "little girl" Don knew so well many years ago, always came "alive" this time of year captivated by the spirit of Christmas. She indulged herself, each day building more excitement, until finally the magical moment arrived with the dawn of Christmas morning!

Embarrassed, Don rushed from the store, his head bowed partly to brunt the wind, but mostly to hide his now misty eyes. He bumped squarely into a burly figure. Looking up, he saw Charlie. They had served on the Salvation Army Advisory Board years ago. Charlie was a widower also, having lost his wife years earlier in an automobile accident. Charlie spoke first. Don muttered, "Charlie," then passed quickly. Finally home, he sank into the overstuffed leather chair, his place of refuge. Staring into the darkness, all the memories of Sharon emerged as they had so many times. Raw emotions flooded the room as if her passing was all happening anew.

Several long days, then a couple long weeks, passed. Don felt locked in time, his mood growing darker like the season that offered less sunlight each passing day.

Late one evening, the telephone's sudden loud ring shattered the stillness that hung like a fog over the apartment. Startled, Don sprang from his recliner. Clearly irritated, he scowled as he turned toward the blaring phone. "Another annoying telemarketer!" he grumbled. Raising the phone, ready with a quick, repulsive response, Don glanced at the caller ID. Oops. It was Charlie.

Small talk followed until Charlie explained that he'd had Don on his mind since their chance encounter in front of Brooks Food Palace. "Anyway, for some reason, a feeling kept nudging me to contact you." Charlie suggested they meet for a cup of coffee at the diner just down the street from Don's apartment. Caught off guard, Don reluctantly agreed.

Locals regarded the diner as a "gathering place." It wasn't much to look at from the outside, or from the inside for that matter. Don crossed its threshold and glanced left and right at the three wooden booths. Most were empty. How many times had he and Sharon slid across those smooth bench seats to let someone join in on their conversation? They'd not come here very often; today Don appreciated that fact. Even so, the booths were a reminder.

He'd forgotten the waitress's name, if he'd ever known it. She asked if he preferred a booth or the counter. She understood why he hadn't sat down when Don quietly said he would be meeting someone.

Maybe Charlie would choose one of the eight swivel stools at the long counter covered in faded yellow Formica. Lately Don had chosen those red plastic cushions a time or two, mostly when he'd groaned because making just one or two cups of coffee in an eight-cup pot never turned out right. He couldn't remember staying for a refill; the whole place reeked of hot grease from too many years of grilled onions, fries, and hamburgers. Today, though, he welcomed the whiff of something predictable but almost unfamiliar from his past.

Where was Charlie? Don glanced at the oversized clock centered on the wall at the far end of the diner. He recognized the "Hank's Appliances" logo on its face without needing to move closer. For decades, several downtown stores had cooperated in mutual promotional freebies like cheap landscape calendars, ballpoint pens, and folded plastic rain scarves tucked tightly inside a plastic sleeve reminding ladies where to shop for clothes. Back then, the long, pointed hands moving around the clock's face made a subtle, tasteful statement about Hank's success before time passed it by, much like the diner's black and white tiled floors that refused to shine.

Old habits die hard, even in retirement. Don still practiced and commended punctuality. Had he misunderstood Charlie? He moved toward one of the two large windows to get a better look down the sidewalk. Ah, yes, little puffs of breath rose between Charlie and another bundled gentleman. Charlie was a retired car salesman. Of course he'd be held up. He saw Charlie's farewell nod followed his hurried steps.

Recalling Charlie's incredible gift of gab brought relief. Don wouldn't have to carry the conversation. Charlie picked a booth without realizing Don had preferred the counter. "Just so you know, Maria, a booth is better for men like us who wake up each morning and wonder if we can go another day without spending money on hearing aids," Charlie joked.

Charlie kept the conversation light, sensing Don's uneasiness. Forty-five minutes later after two cups of coffee, Charlie said he had to go, explaining a busy morning schedule. In departing, he thanked Don and suggested they do this again soon. Don replied "Maybe, Sure!"

As the days passed, Don caught himself recalling their coffee visit, each time experiencing a slight inner warmth. The conversation had provided a nice escape from the continuous mental replay of some many memories shared with Sharon, a respite of sorts from the torment of knowing life would never be the same without her.

Don and Charlie met again in a few days, same diner, same booth! Maria in her high pitch voice hollered, "Hi, Boys!" and flashed a smile.

As the weeks passed, their "coffee visits" became a ritual. Each time Don came away feeling more refreshed, often inspired. Miraculously, Don began taking the lead in conversations as Charlie shared thoughts and probed with questions to draw out pent-up feelings of sorrow and despair. A change was happening in Don's life. A healing was underway. Gradually, facing each day seemed easier. Don was starting to move on in a good and healthy way!

A few days before Christmas, just as they finished their first cup of coffee, Charlie leaned in toward Don and whispered, "I've brought you something!" Glancing around to make sure he wasn't attracting the attention of those close by, Charley slid a brown sack across the table. Don, now leaning forward, carefully reached inside the sack and pulled out a book whose cover simply read, "Journal." Charlie, with a slight grin, hesitantly watched to catch Don's reaction.

Don thumbed the first few pages, absorbed in the pages momentarily partly to hide his surprise, but more to not show a face he was sure broadcasted embarrassment. A few seconds passed as Don collected his thoughts. "Thank... thank you Charlie! This is so nice of you, so unexpected! I didn't bring anything for you, I had no idea..."

Charlie quickly responded, rescuing his friend's dignity. "Oh, nothing expected! If you really feel you need to respond, just drop something in the Salvation Army Red Kettle down the street! That would be more than enough!"

Don hesitated, still staring down at the gift. Finally he raised his eyes to meet Charlie's. "I've never had a journal before, and to be honest, I've never been one to have done much writing!"

Charlie smiled and reached to touch Don's hand. "Journaling doesn't require much experience! All you do is start each entry by writing the day's calendar date, and then just jot down how you feel that day. Also, maybe a few thoughts and perhaps include a blessing that may have come your way. Those days when life seems to beat you down, flip through the pages. You'll be encouraged by the progress you've made. Then give thanks for all God is doing in your life!"

When Don got home, he decided he would sit down and express what he was feeling. He opened the journal, looked at the calendar, and quickly wrote today's month and day. On the next line his pencil tip landed and stopped. Don struggled, staring blankly out the window trying to come up with the right words to capture exactly how he felt. Finally, after what seemed like an hour, a smile broke across his face and he softly uttered, "I feel better!" He simply wrote, "Better," in his journal.

Gradually the words began to come more quickly. They flowed easier than he thought they would. Before long, writing in the journal from Charlie became almost routine. Some days the entries caught a couple of teardrops, but as the year moved on, Don felt himself getting stronger.

Gradually, most memories of Sharon were those made him smile! The journal, and Charlie, became a safe way to connect with his feelings and move on.

Some day, perhaps, someone else will read the journal entry Don made as yet another December rolled around for the widower who no longer dreaded the Christmas season. It reads: "Eventfully hope returns as we emerge from the valley. God equips us to live with this pain that never quite goes away. God comes alongside and accompanies us through our most challenging days and He lights our path through our darkest nights. Beautiful memories fill the void replacing sadness and despair. Our "new normal" enables the return of joy, peace, and the hope that only God can provide, as we celebrate His Son's birth."

58 ~ THE STIRRING

MATTHEW A. POE

Andrew rechecked the thermostat for his small one-bedroom apartment and pushed it up a degree. The chill wasn't all because of the overcast December skies. His efforts to keep this morning's conversations light and non-combative were failing. Maybe he shouldn't have sent the lame text inviting his brother and girlfriend over. He forced his clenched jaw to relax. Steve's latest crude words hung awkwardly in the air.

Janice sounded like she might need some help, but offering to help right now would only make things worse. He'd not met her until about fifteen minutes ago. He'd instantly wondered how this bouncy optimist had ever decided she'd pair up with Steve.

Steve had come in peeved at something. He'd not bothered to initiate the introductions, so Andrew handled that as he took their coats and offered coffee and hot water for instant cocoa. Steve set his six-pack on the counter with a, "You know I don't go anywhere without my best friends," and waved off a glass when Andrew opened the cupboard door.

Janice seemed grateful for the hot chocolate and wrapped her fingers around the cup to warm them. She'd commented on the coziness of the apartment and the assortment of cardboard boxes while Steve's expression negated her assessments.

"Well, Steve, we came to help decorate, so let's get started," Janice said, reaching into a box and pulling out a stringy wad of old silver tinsel. She tossed it at Steve but ducked when he angrily batted it back with a more careless words now hanging in the air.

Andrew noticed Janice's face flush before she headed into the next room where she now noisily struggled to shake out the three-foot artificial tree. How many times had she witnessed Steve's temper? Surely Steve knew better than to take his anger out on a girlfriend. If he weren't my brother, I'd …

Andrew's mind drew a blank. I'd what? Shove him up against the wall? Tell him to grow up, to stop being a jerk, to show respect? To leave? He wanted to yell that it was Christmas, like that would solve everything, or yell that people should try to mend relationships and get along. He shot up a silent prayer, almost a threat, "Lord, You'd better dump a truckload of patience…"

He inhaled and rearranged the old cardboard boxes he'd carried from the closet. He balanced the one with his mom's handwriting on the kitchen's narrow counter between the yellowing refrigerator and beige stove. In uneven letters in black marker, she'd written, "Christmas Decorations, Some Old."

"Oh, that should be interesting," Steve groaned. "We always were the house to behold at Christmastime."

Andrew wouldn't take the bait to rehash failures. "It was what it was." He shrugged and unfolded the cardboard flaps. He knew the wrinkled newspaper's secrets before he lifted out what his fingers grasped. One of Mom's whimsical mice. Nothing a construction worker would buy for his apartment, but they'd belonged to Mom. She'd made them a gift of sorts. He unwrapped the upright plastic mouse and looked around.

"Really, Andrew?"

"What?"

"You're going to put that up?"

Andrew looked at the decoration and then Steve. "Yeah, why?"

Steve popped the top of his beer and let the foam drip wherever it fell. "It's a mouse in a Santa suit."

"Yes, and?"

"We're not kids anymore, Andrew, in case Mom forgot to tell you. Besides, what's a mouse got to do with Christmas?"

"You know, 'All is calm, all is bright, not a creature was stirring, not even a mouse'?"

Steve didn't move. He didn't even blink.

"Mouse? What mouse?" came Janice's cheery voice from the living room. She peeked over Steve's shoulder. "Oh, he's so cute!"

Andrew reached into the box. He pulled out another mouse, this one in a red dress fringed with white. Slipping off its baldhead, like the other mouse, it wore a long, red hat that ended in a white puff. She wore a pair of glasses on the tip of her brown nose. Both mice had oversized ears, large, oval eyes, and buckteeth in a comically smiling mouth.

Janice clapped. "Mr. and Mrs. Mouse Claus!"

"Pantsless," Steve grumbled.

Janice squeezed past Steve and took Mrs. Mouse.

"They're mice," she said. "They don't wear pants."

"But they dress like Santa Claus?"

"Steve, Andrew invited us over to help decorate, not criticize. Where do they go?"

Andrew smiled at Janice. It faded when he saw Steve roll his eyes, frown, then take another gulp of his beer.

"On top of the refrigerator."

"Can I put them up?"

"Sure."

"Yay!" Janice squeezed around Andrew, stood on her tiptoes and grabbed the half loaf of bread and bag of chips from the top of refrigerator. She placed those on the small, cracked countertop next to the sink. Then she set Mrs. Mouse on the refrigerator, and when Andrew handed her Mr. Mouse, she placed him to Mrs. Mouse's left.

"Um, they go the other way around," Andrew said.

"Oh," Janice said, and swapped their positions. "Like that?"

"Angle them a little more toward each other. Yes, perfect."

"Please tell me those things are at least worth something," Steve moaned.

"I looked them up online," Andrew said. "From what I can find out, some guy named Roy Des something made them. They're toy banks handed out in 1970. Best price I saw is $50 for the pair."

"Ridiculous," Steve said. "At least tell me you don't think the song and the poem are one in the same."

"I was joking," Andrew said.

"What are you talking about?" Janice asked.

"My brother, of superior intelligence, is concerned that I have mixed a classic Christmas song with a piece of holiday literature and believe them to be one piece."

Janice stared at Andrew. "What?"

Andrew continued, "When I said, 'All is calm, all is bright, not a creature was stirring, not even a mouse,' the 'All is calm, all is bright,' is from the song *Silent Night*. The other part is from the poem, *A Visit from St. Nicholas*. Most people know it as *'Twas the Night Before Christmas*. I mashed the two together, just to be silly."

"Oh, yeah, *The Night Before Christmas*, I know that," Janice said. "I don't think I've heard *Silent Night*."

"Oh, come on," Steve scoffed. "Everybody's heard that one."

"It's a hymn, Janice," Andrew said, leaning against the counter.

"It's boring," Steve grunted.

Andrew ignored him "It's about the night Jesus was born. It probably sounds strange, but these mice remind me of that."

"The song?"

"About Jesus being born. Every year when our mom put these two mice out on top of the refrigerator, just like you set them, she would say they reminded her of a story about the mouse in the manger."

"Do you really—"

Janice, still on the chair, reached down and pushed her fingers across Steve's mouth. "Shush, I want to hear it," she said.

"Well, it goes something like this," Andrew started. "When Mary and Joseph couldn't find any place to stay in Bethlehem, she ended up having Baby Jesus in a stable. After He was born and Mary had wrapped Him all up, she went to lay Jesus in the manger. Inside, she found a mouse. It had fluffed up the hay and stray fur into a comfortable little bed, but when the mouse saw Jesus, the mouse moved aside. Mary watched what the mouse did, and then placed Jesus in the soft bed. Then, the mouse crawled up by Jesus's neck, curled up, and went to sleep. And Jesus snuggled it."

Janice reached toward the plastic mice, gently touching her fingertips to the ear of Mr. Mouse. The plastic was cool, yet she could feel … something. She leaned over and gazed at the mice for a moment.

"Steve, I thought you said you didn't have any family traditions at Christmas," she said, still touching the mice.

"Not any good ones. No important ones. Anyway, I don't think Mom ever told me that story."

"She did," said Andrew. "You just said it was stupid."

"Well, sounds like it was."

"After Dad died, the story kept getting longer," Andrew said to Janice, ignoring Steve. "More animals would watch. Joseph ended up taking the mouse home with them, all sorts of things like that. I wish I could remember more of the story. I think last year, before she died, it took Mom about half an hour to tell it. But at least I remember the important part."

"What's that?" Janice asked.

"That Jesus was born."

"What a joke!" Steve said. "Christmas isn't some holy season, goodwill toward men and all that. It's just a time for people to be greedy, ask for expensive stuff, and get ticked off when they don't get it."

"Yes, Steve, I know," Andrew sighed. "You've said it all before. And, yes, that's what it's become, but that's not what it's supposed to be."

Janice stood, arms crossed, looking at Steve. "You never told me your mom and dad were gone."

"We've only been together a couple months, Jan."

"But, I've told you lots of things about my family."

"Doesn't matter."

"Yes, it does," she said.

Steve slammed his beer on the counter. Golden liquid and foam sprayed up onto the box of decorations. "No," he growled, "it doesn't!"

"Guys, I invited you over to help me decorate, not to fight."

"You're just trying to make yourself feel good," Steve retorted. "That's why you told us to come over."

"No," Andrew said through his teeth, "I hadn't seen you in a couple months and I hadn't met Janice." He drew in a deep breath. "I hoped we could just have a little fun."

"Bull. You just want to rub it in my face."

Andrew was puzzled. "What are you talking about?"

"Why'd you get them?" Steve asked.

"Get what?"

Steve waved his hand toward the refrigerator, casting an angry glance at Mr. and Mrs. Mouse.

"The mice?" Andrew asked. "I thought you said they're stupid."

"No, I said they're ridiculous."

"What do you care?" Andrew said, blinking in confusion. "You got the house and most of the money. What are you saying? You want *them*, now too?"

"Don't be an idiot. I just want to know why Mom gave them to you."

"You knew she left them to me," Andrew said, slowly. "You were there when we met with the lawyer."

Steve stepped toward Andrew. "I know what you got. I want to know why she gave *those things* to you."

It was Andrew's turn to take a step, a half step, toward his brother. "Because I was there."

"What's that supposed to mean?"

"Steve, come on," Janice said, laying her hand on his arm. "I think you two need to calm down and listen to -"

"Don't," Steve spat, pulling away.

"Yeah, don't Janice," Andrew said. "It's not worth you getting into the middle of it. And it means just what I said, brother, dear. I was there, after Dad died."

"Don't try to say I didn't help Mom."

"I'm saying I was there, just there, with her. I was there, at Christmas time, when Mom decorated. I helped her get the boxes from the attic and watched as she pulled out each decoration and ornament. I listened to the stories about each one. Listened to the stories about Dad."

For a moment, the only sound in the kitchen was the plink-plink of the leaky faucet. Steve threw the half-empty beer can toward the sink. It clanged off the backsplash, bounced into the sink, and then out, onto the floor. Foam and beer sputtered onto the worn linoleum.

No one moved. Then, glaring from Andrew to Janice, Steve's eyes began to glisten. He finally jerked around and stormed out of the apartment.

Janice was the first to breathe. She looked down at the oozing spill on the kitchen floor. "Do you have paper towels or something?" she asked softly.

"It can't make the floor look any worse," Andrew said, staring at the empty space where his brother had just stood.

Janice studied Andrew's face. "Are you all right?"

"I'm not sure what just happened," he said, shaking his head.

Janice looked from the spilled beer to the mice and then at Andrew. "I knew Steve has a temper, but is he always like this?"

"No," Andrew said, thinking. "Something was different this time."

"You mean he's getting worse?"

"No, I think he's getting better. Usually he just rolls his eyes and walks away. He had tears in his eyes."

"He threw his beer and slammed the door."

"I know," Andrew said. "Something's changed. We need to go find him."

"Really?"

"Yes."

"Why?"

"Because …" Andrew paused. "Because, as difficult as it is, I love my brother. Let's get our coats on."

Janice put on her coat and started to pull her mittens out of the pocket. "Do you really believe the baby Jesus story?"

"Well, not the part about the mouse."

Janice smiled. "No, not the mouse, but Jesus, being born, all that. You believe?"

Andrew smiled, "'For God so loved the world that He gave His one and only Son that whoever believes in Him shall not perish but have eternal life.' That's in the Bible. John 3:16. Oh, yes, I believe. That's why I want to find Steve."

"Okay, I'll go, but only if you tell me more along the way. And if we can clean this up, first."

Andrew turned and looked at Janice sideways. "Are you a neat freak?"

"I can't stand messes."

"Then why are you with my brother?" Andrew asked with a wry smile.

"Let's just clean this up and go find him."

THE END

"The first thing Andrew did was to find his brother Simon and tell him, 'We have found the Messiah (that is, 'the Christ'). And he brought him to Jesus." (John 1:41-42 NIV)

59 ~ COMING HOME

JONITA MULLINS

"Mother, you know I'd love to come home for Christmas," James said over the phone as he leaned back in the expensive leather chair. "But things just haven't worked out for me to get away this year." His voice sounded sheepish, like a little boy who had gotten caught doing something he shouldn't.

His mother, Martha Perkins, could tell a lot from his voice. She could tell that someone else was in the office with him because he called her "Mother." Usually he still called her "Mama," unless there was someone else around. Probably it was one of his associates in the law firm, or maybe it was that girlfriend of his, Susan. He'd been spending a lot of time with her lately.

"But the whole family is going to be here, Jimmy," Martha said. "Jerry's coming in from school and Cecelia and Robert and the kids are driving up from Atlanta. Everybody's going to make it for the service on Christmas Eve and then there'll be a big dinner at your grandpa's on Christmas Day. Don't you think you could make it at least for that?"

"I'm afraid not, Mother," James said as he squirmed in his chair. He could face a judge, jury, and the toughest D.A. in Chicago with few qualms, but he hated to be on the opposite side of an argument with his mother. And he was embarrassed that Susan was hearing his not exactly truthful answers.

"It's the day before Christmas Eve," James tried to explain. "All flights would have been booked for weeks. I couldn't hope to get a ticket home at this late date."

Mrs. Perkins listened quietly. She knew what she was hearing was just an excuse. But she had promised herself that she wouldn't nag. "All right, Jimmy," she said at last. "But I hate to think of you spending Christmas by yourself."

"I won't be alone, Mother," James said. "Susan and I are spending Christmas together."

"Oh," Martha said. She wasn't upset that James wanted to spend Christmas with Susan. But she had felt for a long time that her son was reluctant to bring her home to meet everyone. Intuitively, she feared James didn't want Susan to see his poor country home in the mountains of northern Georgia.

"I'll call Grandpa about noon on Christmas," James said, "and talk to everyone then, ok?"

"Well, all right," his mother said. "You have a good Christmas."

"Merry Christmas, Ma-, Mother."

"God bless you, Son."

"God bless you too, Mother," James said as he leaned with his ear just above the phone on his desk so he could hang up before more explanations were required. He didn't realize that he heaved a great sigh of relief until he glanced up at Susan and saw the look in her deep brown eyes. She could look at him just like his mother and it had the very same effect of making him feel guilty.

⌘

Susan and James ate an early dinner at his apartment on Christmas Eve. While a light snow fell outside, they sat in front of the fireplace. With only a little coaxing, Susan had persuaded James to open their gifts this afternoon instead of waiting for Christmas Day. James hadn't needed much persuasion. He was anxious to see Susan's reaction to the gift he had bought for her.

Susan opened the long slender box to reveal a beautiful choker-length strand of pearls. They glistened against their velvet nest.

"Oh, they're beautiful, James," she said and held them up for him to fasten around her neck. They caught the light of the fireplace and shone against her dark skin.

"Now you open your present," Susan said.

James fingered the bright package she handed him. It was long and flat and he had no idea what could be inside. He tore the paper away and pulled out two airline tickets.

"Great," James said, not looking too closely at the tickets. He assumed they were to Denver since he and Susan had planned to go skiing in a few weeks. "I'll have to get my skis waxed."

"I don't think so," Susan said. "They don't do much skiing in Atlanta."

"Atlanta?"

"Yes, you know, it's south of Cutter Mountain, Georgia, home of James Perkins the famous attorney-at-law."

"How did you get tickets?"

"I've had them for weeks," Susan explained. "In the two years that I've known you, you haven't gone home once. Every time I mention your home, you change the subject."

"I didn't think you'd be interested."

"I'm interested in everything about you, James," Susan said. "And I think it's time I met your family. That is, if you want me to."

"Susan," James said slowly, "my family is just simple country folks. They live way out in the sticks in the foothills of the *Smokies* in a town that doesn't even have a post office."

"So? Do you think I'm a snob?"

"No, of course not," James answered. "I just wasn't sure you'd feel comfortable there."

"I think you're the snob, James. You've been away from home too long."

"Maybe you're right," James agreed reluctantly.

"Come on," Susan said, looking at her watch. "We have one hour for you to get packed and then get to the airport. My bags are already in the car."

⌘

The airplane taxied to the end of the runway at the Atlanta airport. The evening was cold and clear and a full moon made the frost on the ground glisten. Atlanta hadn't seen any snow yet this winter, but in the mountains a couple of inches had fallen.

James and Susan picked up their bags, loaded them into a rental car and headed north. As they sped along the highway, James pointed out old familiar sites. In less time than seemed possible they were turning off the highway onto the winding road that led up to Cutter Mountain. Here a light wet snow lay like a cake frosting, white and gleaming in the moonlight.

When they reached the county road that ran through the small community of Cutter Mountain, the snow hadn't even been cleared. Everything looked quiet and isolated as if time had stood still since James had last been there.

"Everybody will be at church," James said.

The late service on Christmas Eve was a long-standing tradition. In fact, they could see the light spilling from the windows of the church in the distance.

As they pulled into the churchyard and got out of the car, they could hear the congregation singing. They crunched across the snow to the last refrain of "Silent Night."

James took Susan's hand and they slipped quietly into the building and sat on the back pew. While they joined in singing "O Come All Ye Faithful," James looked around at the familiar room. The scarred wooden pews, the out-of-tune upright piano, the faded picture of the Good Shepherd, all stirred his memories. He found them sweet and good, not bitter as he had feared.

He saw his mother sitting on the front pew with a row of wiggling angels. As always, Mrs. Perkins was in charge of the nativity play the children would perform. The rest of James' family was scattered throughout the congregation.

It wasn't until his mother stood to shepherd the shepherds to their places that she realized James was there. Her eyes lit up and she smiled at him. He slowly returned her smile.

He squeezed Susan's hand in a silent *thank you*. She had given him the best of Christmas gifts. Having once escaped the poverty, he had been afraid to come back, lest it engulf him again. He found he came back not to poverty, but to great wealth—to home, family, and faith.

As the little angels sang a welcome to the Baby in the manger, James felt the peace the angels announced. At last for him Christmas could once again mean . . . coming home.

60 ~ A GIFT FROM JOSEPH

MARILYN BOONE

"You're crazy, Jenna Hughes."

"Since you're coming with me, Haley Hughes, then you must be just as crazy," Jenna shot back with a gleam of challenge in her eyes.

Their mother shook her head. "If I didn't know better, I'd think you girls were still in high school. A lot of snow has fallen today for you two to be walking to church."

"But that's what makes it perfect!" Jenna couldn't contain her excitement. "It's Christmas Eve snow."

"Well, don't forget the lantern then," Mrs. Hughes said, buttoning her coat and wrapping a scarf around her neck. "Your father has Dominick loaded in the trailer, and I'm off now to help the angels with their wings."

"Mom, are you sure having a live donkey in the pageant is a good idea? Remember last year?" Haley's eyebrows rose and the two of them erupted in laughter.

Mrs. Hughes paused, "Poor Dominick."

"Poor Jeremy," Haley countered. "He was the shepherd standing right behind Dominick, and in the middle of *Joy to the World* of all times."

Jenna felt her festive mood diminish as their laughter resumed and she remembered why she wasn't home last Christmas. It was because of Robert, the boyfriend who insisted a ski trip with his family was the quintessential way to spend the holidays. She had never been more miserable.

Mrs. Hughes opened the door to leave. "If you change your mind, I'm sure Brandon wouldn't mind picking you up."

The door had no sooner closed than Jenna sensed her sister's gaze and knew the subject couldn't be avoided any longer. "How is Brandon doing these days? Being a single parent can't be easy."

"Jeremy is a great kid and Brandon's a great father," Haley answered, hesitating before she continued, "He asks about you, Jen. He still cares."

"Well, he sure didn't waste time finding someone else. I wasn't in college a year before he was married and had a baby on the way."

"What did you expect? You all but pushed him into Shelly Hastings' arms, making it very clear that life on a Christmas tree farm wasn't for you. I recall you were going to rescue the world."

Haley's words stung. She had been the one needing rescue. Six years away from home and all she had to show for it were an ex-boyfriend and an English degree. Jenna looked at her sister. "I was sorry to hear about Shelly's accident."

Haley took in a deep breath. "It was bound to happen. A couple of drinks at Casey's Den were all it took before Shelly would start saying she didn't care if she smelled another fir tree ever again. It's sad, but she finally got her wish."

Jenna frowned. "Couldn't Brandon stop her?"

"He tried," Haley defended him. "But he was busy protecting Jeremy and literally growing a business."

Jenna was more thoughtful when she spoke again. "I hope he finds the right person someday. He deserves to be happy."

"You ought to see all the work he's done to the farm." Haley nodded toward the living room. "Just look at our beautiful tree."

Haley was right. It was beautiful. Jenna walked over close enough to touch her nose to its needles. "Who wouldn't want to smell Christmas all year long?"

The instant the question left her mouth, Jenna knew the conclusion Haley would jump to. "Forget it, Sis. Brandon is a father now, and that changes everything."

"It doesn't have to," Haley pressed.

"It does if I'm being honest with myself. I don't know if I could love someone else's child as much as I would love my own, and that wouldn't be fair." Jenna bristled at the harshness of her own words but wanted to put an end to her sister's notions.

Haley turned away. "We should get ready to leave. I'll get the lantern while you change into more suitable clothes. It's obvious you haven't lived in this part of the country for a while."

Jenna found a pair of boots and a wool sweater to wear underneath her jacket then stepped outside with Haley onto the fresh crystal landscape. She knew by her sister's silence she had upset her.

"I've missed walking in the snow," Jenna said after some time had passed with hearing only the crunching sound of their footsteps.

Haley's response was soft. "I'm glad you're home, Jenna. I just want you to be happy, too."

"I know." Jenna smiled at her, though the walk was turning out to be another painful reminder of last year's ski trip.

She hadn't been nearly as skilled a skier as Robert or his parents, and spent most of her afternoons inside the condominium or on the lower slopes skiing alone. To be fair, Robert offered to stay with her once, but by then she preferred her own private pity party, wallowing in the disappointing absence of decorations and fresh baked cookies.

The closer they got to the church, the more Jenna shivered at the possibility of seeing Brandon again. Would he even want to talk to her if she did? So many years had passed. She wasn't sure what either of them would say.

They had just come around the last bend when Jenna slowed down to take in the sight ahead. She had forgotten how beautiful the white clapboard church was this time of year, with its tall steeple and the flicker of candles glowing from every window. Wreaths and garlands of fresh greens adorned every post and door, and a prelude of carols accompanied the festive welcome to come inside.

"What's going to happen when Miss Woodbury can't play the organ anymore?" Jenna asked.

Haley laughed. "Maybe you could learn how. You were always a better piano player than me. That is if you were ever to move back to Kings Valley."

"Are you insinuating I might end up a spinster like Miss Woodbury?" Jenna laughed, too, though she didn't find the prospect particularly funny.

By then they had climbed the steps and walked through the front door. Jenna waved to her mother who looked as if she had earned her own set of angel wings, but so far there was no sign of Brandon. She didn't know if she was disappointed or relieved.

Haley led the way past several pews before finding space in one next to the aisle. Once they were seated she whispered, "Jeremy is playing Joseph this year."

Jenna suddenly became as restless as the little angels she had seen waiting to make their entrance. "I'm going to see if Dad needs help with Dominick."

"But the pageant is about to start," Haley reminded her.

"I'll be right back." Jenna exited through the side door into the hallway, only to stop as soon as she turned the corner.

A man leaning over a little boy looked her way. "Jenna?"

Jenna was unable to move as he straightened up and walked toward her. It was Brandon all right, but he looked so much stronger and confident than she remembered.

"Hi Brandon," Jenna stammered, hoping she didn't sound as awkward as she felt. She couldn't decide whether to shake his hand or give him a hug, so she did neither.

"I didn't know you were coming home for Christmas this year." His eyes searched hers as he smiled. "You look great. College life must have agreed with you."

"Thanks." Jenna wasn't about to go into all the reasons it actually hadn't and shifted her attention toward the boy whose blue eyes and dark hair were like his father's. "You must be Jeremy."

"I'm sorry," Brandon apologized. "Jeremy, this is Miss Hughes. She's a friend from high school."

They had been much more than friends, she thought as she extended her hand to shake Jeremy's.

"You can call me, Jenna, if it's all right with your father." Jenna glanced at Brandon for his approval then looked back to Jeremy. "I understand you're going to be Joseph in the pageant."

Jeremy gave her a worried nod.

"Jeremy's having second thoughts about leading Mary up the aisle on Dominick, especially after what happened last year," Brandon explained.

Jenna chuckled. "So I heard." She knelt down, eye level with Jeremy. "Did you know Dominick and I grew up together?"

Jeremy's eyes brightened as he shook his head.

"Well, I happen to know a secret that will help Dominick be on his best behavior. Would you like me to show you?" she asked him.

Jeremy looked up at his father.

Brandon's eyebrows rose. "You'll have to be quick. It's almost time for the pageant to start."

"Come with me then, Joseph," Jenna said, turning to guide Jeremy down the rest of the hallway.

Brandon started to follow when Jenna stopped him. "I think it's better if only Joseph knows the secret for now. Why don't you go ahead into the church?"

Brandon's gaze shifted to his son. "I'll be okay," Jeremy said.

Jenna gave Brandon a quick wink before she took Jeremy to where Dominick and the girl who was playing Mary were waiting alongside Jenna's father.

"Dad, do you still keep peppermints around for Dominick?"

Mr. Hughes rubbed his chin. "I reckon I quit that when you quit showing him."

Jenna thought for a moment. "Hold on, Jeremy."

She ran outside to her dad's pickup and opened the glove box, figuring it hadn't been cleaned out in just as long. It was where she used to hide the peppermints in case she ever ran out. Jenna dug her hand beneath the papers, checking each corner. Hope was dwindling when her fingers ran across a hard disc-shaped object. Jenna pulled to get it unstuck, then grinned as she smelled the familiar candy. It was old and sticky but Dominick wouldn't care.

Jenna hurried back inside, untwisting the plastic wrapper as she went, and quickly rubbed the peppermint up and down the length of Dominick's lead rope. It was a ritual that had always brought her good luck. "There, that should keep him calm."

She then took Jeremy's hands in hers. "Don't worry. You're going to be the best Joseph ever."

Jenna slipped back into the pew beside Haley, catching Brandon's glance from a couple of rows up. She gave him an assuring smile.

All eyes were on Jeremy as he began leading Mary up the aisle to Bethlehem and the inn. He couldn't have looked more proud as he passed by them while Jenna held her breath. She released a huge sigh of relief when the pageant ended without any incidents.

After the last carol had been sung, she and Haley followed the crowd into the fellowship hall where a line had formed to get refreshments. Jenna was about to pick up a cup of wassail when she felt a tug on her coat. She turned around to see Jeremy grinning up at her.

"The secret worked," he said.

Jenna laughed. "Yes, it did. Dominick loves the smell of peppermint, but he loves having friends even more. Maybe you can come visit him sometime."

Jeremy threw both his arms around her, causing Jenna to respond in kind.

Once he pulled away, Jenna looked at Brandon who was standing off to the side.

"Maybe you can visit the Christmas tree farm, too," he said.

"I would like that," Jenna answered, doing her best to ignore the medley of feelings stirring inside her.

She was thankful to return home a short time later, anxious to change into her flannel pajamas and go to bed. After wrapping herself in warm blankets, Jenna closed her eyes, hoping sleep would come easily, but it didn't. Memories of Brandon kept flashing through her mind as well as pictures of Jeremy with Dominick, playing the role of Joseph.

*Joseph...*Jenna's eyes flew open, seeming to have heard the name spoken by a voice outside her thoughts. "Joseph," she repeated aloud.

Lying in the darkness, Jenna reflected more on this man who became Mary's husband. Not only did Joseph have the faith and courage to love Mary, he was also the perfect example of a father to Jesus, a child that wasn't his. Jenna's heart pounded with the realization of how wrong she had been. It had only taken minutes for Jeremy to take up residence in her heart. Jenna knew how much she could love him, whether he was her flesh and blood or not. But there was more. She also knew the feelings she had tried to deny having for Brandon were still there, as strong and real as they had ever been.

Jenna closed her eyes again, this time with a smile. She looked forward to waking up and opening gifts with her family, but it was the gift that wouldn't be wrapped with paper or bows that she anticipated the most. It was the one Joseph had given her...the one waiting for her at a Christmas tree farm.

An Excerpt from . . .

61 ~ PIECES ON EARTH

CATHY BRYANT

Chapter 1

Liv finished filling out the necessary paperwork in the medical clinic waiting room, doing her best to keep her fears at bay.

She rose to her feet and carried the clipboard with the completed paperwork to the receptionist. The harried woman took the clipboard without so much as a glance her way. "Have a seat. A nurse will call you back momentarily."

Liv trudged back to the worn gray chairs and slumped into one of them, once more cognizant of her reason for being here. October marked her second month without her period. For most women her age, that would be a sign of promising things to come, but no such luck in her case. She'd known since her daughter's birth that having more children just wasn't in the cards for her---a fact that made Chesney's life even more miraculous.

She gnawed the inside of her lip and watched a little boy--probably about two years old--playing on the floor with a toy car. Without warning, the fear returned, bringing with it only one thought. Was it possible that she'd somehow inherited the gene that lead to the ovarian cancer that claimed her grandmother's life? Was that the reason for her current symptoms?

Liv pressed her lips together and forced her thoughts to happier ones. How wonderful it would be to add a fourth member to their clan. Chesney would make such a great big sister, and Jeff would be ecstatic to have another child. Since being promoted to lieutenant a few months ago, he had qualified for a stateside assignment as an instructor pilot at

Pensacola NAS. How wonderful would it be to be able to raise a child with his or her parent actually around to help out? Even the few short months of having her daddy at home had made a huge difference in Chesney.

A pent-up sigh whooshed from her lungs. This current line of thought was landing her nowhere except in the dumps. There wouldn't be another baby. She grabbed her large sack of a purse and rummaged inside until she found an old envelope. Forcing the baby blues away, she started a to-do list of things to accomplish for her family's first Christmas together since before Chesney was born.

Get the Christmas shopping done. Well, that was a no-brainer. But this year it was especially important, since they'd also be buying gifts for nieces, nephews, siblings, aunts, and uncles. How fun it would be to have both sides of the family all together again in the mountain cabin vacation rental her mother had located online.

Now happy thoughts wound their way through her insides. Liv leaned her head back against the Plexiglas partition and allowed the happiness to wander unchecked. Warm sweaters, cups of cocoa, a gigantic tree stuffed with presents, laughter of loved ones, and fluffy white snow.

Though she loved the sunny weather of Pensacola where Jeff was stationed, during the holidays she always yearned for the cold weather and snow of her Colorado upbringing. This year it would finally become a reality.

She straightened in her seat, checked the clock above the receptionist window, and returned to her list. *Buy Chesney some cold weather clothing.* Hmm, maybe she could order a ski bib online, since there was very little to no chance that she'd find one in Pensacola.

One thought led to another, and Liv scribbled as quickly as possible, unwilling to let even the smallest detail escape. A few minutes later, she brushed some escaped frizzy hair from her face and once more scanned her list. Yeah, that should do it. Now if she could just get these health concerns out of the way so she could concentrate on more pleasant tasks.

Liv glanced at the clock once more. Unbelievable. She'd been here for a half hour already. At this rate, she'd never make it to Chesney's preschool in time to pick her up. She grabbed her cell phone and hit speed dial for Darcy, one of many military wives in her group who all looked out for each other.

Her friend picked up immediately. "Hi Liv. What's up?"

"My blood pressure."

Darcy's contagious giggle sounded through the phone. "Let me guess. You're still waiting to see the doctor."

"How'd you guess?"

"Umm, 'cause I've been there and done that. Need me to pick up Ches?"

"Yeah, if you don't mind. And if a miracle occurs and I get out of here in time, I'll shoot you a text."

"Sounds good."

Liv had just dropped the phone back into her purse, when a short blond nurse in pink scrubs called her name from the doorway that lead to the exam rooms. She followed the nurse through the door where the dreaded scales awaited. After getting off the scales, fresh resolve took root in Liv's mind to cut back on carbs and lose those ten extra pounds that had plagued her since Chesney was born. Four years was way too long to lug around the unwanted weight. She followed the woman down the hallway and dutifully entered the room to which she motioned.

The nurse smiled and pulled the door toward the closed position. "Dr. Amy will be with you soon."

Liv perched on the edge of the exam table, once more on pins and needles about the potential problem. *Lord, please let me be okay, and please, please, please, don't let this affect our Christmas plans.*

The exam hadn't taken long, but Dr. Amy seemed preoccupied as she asked Liv question after question. In the end, the doctor had done nothing but order urine and blood tests. Now came the worst part. The waiting. Liv took a cleansing breath and wiped sweaty palms on her Capri pants.

As if on cue, the door opened, and the doctor entered, closing the door behind her. "Well, I think we have your diagnosis." Dr. Amy wore an enigmatic expression as she took a seat on a rolling stool in the exam room.

Liv swallowed to hopefully relieve her mouth of the immediate dryness. Was this news she was prepared to hear? And if her recent symptoms had to do with the "C" word that plagued her family, did she really want to know? She exhaled a quick puff of air through pursed lips. "Okay. And?"

A brilliant smile broke out on the middle-aged doctor's face. "You, my dear, are pregnant."

Her jaw dropped. "But how is that even possible? I thought—"

"According to your previous doctor's records, there was always the remote chance, Liv." Dr. Amy checked the file folder in her hands.

"I know, but the odds—"

"--were definitely not in your favor."

Liv allowed the news to truly sink in, and the smile Dr. Amy wore transferred to her own face. "I'm going to have another baby." The words came out in hushed wonder. Chesney and Jeff would both be thrilled, especially since they'd all given up hope of it ever happening. She ran fingers through her hair, partly to curb unruly strands, but mostly just to have something to do with her hands that had gone all flighty as soon as the doctor broke the news. "How far along am I?"

"Just a few weeks. For a due date, I'd say an Independence Day baby."

She gave her head a shake. This was the perfect gift for Jeff for their first

Christmas together in several years. Already, a date with Pinterest loomed in her plans for the immediate future. There had to be a unique and Christmas-y way to pull off the baby announcement to both her husband and their families. "Wow. I'm still trying to wrap my head around this."

Dr. Amy laughed. "That's understandable, but I'm sure it will get real soon enough." The woman's face sobered a bit. "Not to worry you or anything, but with your medical history, you will need to be especially careful."

Liv nodded. That was to be expected. Chesney hadn't made it full term, but at least she'd made it long enough to survive, even if it had meant an extended hospital stay.

The doctor stood, opened the door, and faced Liv once more. "Be sure you stop by the front desk on your way out to schedule your next appointment. I'll see you in about a month."

A few minutes later, Liv stood outside in the beautiful Florida sunshine, her heart as free as the seagulls who cried out their typical sea breeze joy. One would never guess it was October by the balmy temperature. A fact that didn't bother her in the least. Because come December, she and Jeff and Chesney would be up high in the mountains of Colorado, surrounded by their families and crystal white snow.

The years of struggling to make it through another Christmas alone entered her thoughts, but she forcefully shook her head. Not this year. And with Jeff now in a training position, hopefully never again.

Liv checked her watch. Just enough time to pick up Chesney from school, after she sent Darcy a quick text.

Chapter 2

Once back at the house, Liv looked on as her daughter scaled the kitchen island barstool and scooted around until she sat facing Liv in the kitchen.

Liv spread peanut butter on one half of the bread slice and grape jelly on the other half. "I've been meaning to ask you about the Bible stories Daddy's been telling you at bedtime. Do you like the new Bible story book Grandma Hope sent?" Liv smiled as she thought of her mother. Though generally quiet and retiring, as well as diminutive in stature, the woman's faith was larger than life. And when it came to her grandchildren knowing about God, she left no stone unturned. Her mom had rightfully earned the title of faith warrior for their families, determined that all of her grandkids would be with her in heaven some day. Liv folded the bread and slid the sandwich plate across the counter toward her daughter, waiting for an answer.

Chesney picked up the sandwich and took a big bite, nodding her head at the same time.

"Yeah."

"What are the stories about?"

Speaking around bites of sandwich, her daughter answered. "Well, there was one about King Daniel."

"You mean King David."

Her daughter's face went blank, and she stopped chewing momentarily. "I thought David was the one in the fiery furnace."

"No, that would be Shadrach, Meshach, and Abednego."

"Oh, those three guys."

Liv couldn't help the smile that flitted to her lips.

"So those three guys were in the fiery furnace and the lion's den?" Chesney had her head cocked to one side, her dark red wavy hair dangling down.

Now Liv laughed outright. "No, Daniel was in the lion's den."

Chesney licked a blob of peanut butter and grape jelly from her fingers. "They all get tangled up in my head." She finished off the sandwich and chewed, once more talking around the food. "Can I go play in the backyard?"

"Yes, you may."

As she watched her daughter scuttle to the sliding glass doors and out into the sunny yard, Liv considered her daughter's words. Yes, it was good that Chesney understood the individual meaning from each story, but her daughter was missing the bigger picture. Liv skewed her lips to one side. Somehow she had to find a way--not to relay a bunch of unrelated stories--but to tie them all together for her young daughter, so she got a good grasp on the overall message of the good news of God. After all, knowing her mother, Grandma Hope would probably give each of her grandkids a pop quiz at Christmas.

Liv finished a quick clean-up of the kitchen, washed and dried her hands, and then checked to make sure Chesney was still in the backyard. Her daughter played happily in the sand box Jeff had built for her this past summer. Feeling free and lighthearted at all that had transpired that day, Liv snatched up her tablet and moved to the sofa to check out baby announcement ideas on Pinterest.

Later that night, after bath time, Liv approached Jeff, who sat at the dining room table reading the newspaper. She'd been especially careful not to be too exuberant, or her detail-oriented husband would know in a heartbeat that something was up. "Jeff, if you don't mind, I think I'll switch things up with Chesney's bedtime story."

He looked up at her, a slight furrow between his dark eyebrows. "Was I not doing it right?"

Liv laughed. "You were doing it just fine, but I want to try an approach that will hopefully help her see the big picture of the Bible. You on board with that, sailor?"

A grin popped on her husband's face at the naval terminology. "Sure. Want me in there with you?"

"Always." She sent a teasing wink and headed down the hallway to their daughter's room, her ever-helpful hubby on her heels.

A few seconds later, they all lounged on Chesney's bed, leaned up against the frame, with their daughter cradled between them. Liv reached for the Bible she'd placed on the nightstand. "Time for a bedtime story."

Chesney looked up at her like she'd lost her mind. "That's a big story."

Jeff laughed out loud. "The biggest story of all time." He tickled Chesney under her chin until she giggled and ducked away from him.

Liv's heart immediately fluttered. He'd always been a great dad, in spite of his frequent tours of duty. God, thank You for this new baby for all of us, but especially for Jeff. Liv tried to speak in a normal voice. "And it's a story we're a part of." She smiled down at Chesney.

The statement had the intended effect. "We're in the story?" Chesney's eyebrows crinkled in a comical way.

"Yes. But the part I'm going to tell you tonight is about God and the very first man and woman."

Chesney's face brightened. "I know this story. Daddy told it to me not too long ago. God made the world and everything that was in it, then put Adam and Even in the garden of Even."

"You mean the garden of Eden?" Liv over-pronounced the "d" so Chesney would get it right.

"Oh, okay. That place."

Jeff leaned down near their daughter's face. "But do you know how God made the world?"

Chesney lifted wiggling fingers high in the air, her face overly dramatic. "Alacajamkazoo. And poof, there it was."

Liv giggled. "Well, not quite. All God had to do was say what He wanted and it happened. He said, 'Let there be light,' and there was light."

Their daughter's eyes were wide with wonder. "That's amazing. Is that how he created Adam and Eve, too?"

Jeff joined in. "No. The Bible says God stooped down and made Adam by shaping him out of the dirt."

The expression that landed on Chesney's face clearly revealed that she found that idea totally preposterous. "Like a mud pie?"

"No, silly." Liv opened her Bible to Genesis and read the passage directly from the Bible.

"And what about Eve? Did God make her out of dirt, too?"

"When God saw that Adam was lonely, he put Adam to sleep, took out one of his ribs, and created the woman." Jeff spoke the words reverently, then looked up at Liv with a gleam in his eyes. "Adam was very happy about having a helper."

Liv's stomach did a quick somersault. The good news she hid inside threatened to spill out on the spot. She caught a quick breath and captured her daughter's attention. "But what is really cool is that God made the garden first, and He included everything that Adam and Eve would need to live and be happy. He made it perfect just for them."

"So they could live happily ever after just like us." With those words, Chesney wiggled down under the covers and smiled up at her parents. "Good night, Adam and Eve."

All of them shared a laugh, and after good night kisses, both Liv and Jeff laughed all the way out of the room.

Her eyes a-twinkle, Liv handed the Bible to Jeff as he closed the door behind them. "Here you go, Adam. Put that away for me, will you?"

Chapter 3

Later that same week, Liv snatched one of Jeff's bright white t-shirts from the laundry basket and folded it. Just as she laid it on the stack of other t-shirts, the bedroom door opened and Jeff stepped inside, a beleaguered expression on his face. Liv reached into the basket for another piece of clean laundry. "You're home early. Everything okay?"

He didn't speak, but strode into the master bathroom and closed the door behind him. A second later, from within the bathroom, water spewed from the faucet. Then the faucet went silent and the door opened, the grim look still firmly implanted on her husband's face.

His expression brought on a moment of panic inside of Liv, but determined to not let her fears get the best of her, she took a cleansing breath and motioned to the bed beside her. "Okay, mister, park it, and tell me what's going on."

Jeff dropped his weight onto the bed, his upper lip pulled between his teeth and his gaze averted. Finally he released a heavy sigh. His lips clamped into a thin line, and his head shook from side to side, like he wasn't quite sure what to say. Or how to say it.

"You're officially starting to scare me, Jeff. Spill it."

He made eye contact, enough for her to see the storm in the hazel eyes that matched Chesney's. "You're not going to like it. I don't want to tell you."

Liv took a seat on the bed on the other side of the basket, her heart pounding so hard she could feel it in her temples. She closed her eyes, already trying to come to grips with the news he was about to deliver. "You're being deployed."

Jeff's silence was the only affirmation she needed.

The room grew deathly quiet, the air so thick it was palpable.

With shaky breaths and pinched lips, Liv did all she could to control the rising tide of white-hot anger within. All their plans. Plans they'd made, assured that they could finally have a white Christmas together as a family. Then in a move that surprised even her, she hurled the laundry basket to the floor with a guttural scream. "You told me that being an instructor would keep this from happening."

"I thought it would. But the Navy needs some experienced pilots for an upcoming mission."

Tears now coursed, unchecked, down Liv's face. "When?"

"It's a quicker than normal turnaround."

"When?" She nailed him down with her angry gaze.

His Adam's apple bobbed briefly. "Next week." His gaze shifted downward. He released a measured breath between protruding lips, then met her angry glare once more. "They're telling us this one could be especially dangerous."

"Afghanistan again?" The words sounded as though from the deep recesses of her heart, dredging up all-too familiar fears.

Jeff swallowed hard and nodded.

Something inside broke. So much for their plans for a white Christmas in Colorado with their family. So much for her special surprise. So much for having Jeff home safe and sound, with no cause to worry about anything but how well the trainees accepted his instruction. With fisted hands, she swiped away tears that leaked from her eyes. "Well, you're just going to have to tell them no. We've already made plans for Christmas. We haven't had a Christmas together in years, and this one was supposed to be special, back in Colorado with our family."

His eyes held incredible sorrow. "Liv, you knew when you married me that—"

"Yes, but I thought it was different now." Liv cut him off with her poison-laced words. She'd thought that this year would be better. She raised both hands to her head, clutched handfuls of hair made more frizzy by the unrelenting humidity and closed her eyes against demons within. This was all more than she could handle at the moment. Propelled to action by the news that had ruined everything, Liv jumped to her feet and ran from the room, slamming the door behind her so hard that one of the wedding photographs hanging in the hallway crashed to the tile floor, where the frame and glass shattered into pieces.

With the ache in her heart also weighing down her shoulders and dispensing tears down her cheeks, Liv stooped to pick up the photo before the glass marred the portrait, overwhelmed by one thought. The broken frame was the perfect analogy for her life. One minute she'd been on top of the world, happily planning her family's white Christmas and life-changing announcement of a new baby. Then in the next moment, she knelt among nothing but the broken pieces of her now-shattered dreams.

The week preceding Jeff's departure flew way too quickly. In previous deployments they'd had several weeks to prepare, but because of the rush of this particular mission, everything had been crammed into one lousy and pain-ridden week. Physical exhaustion had become the standard mode of operation. In the midst of all the details of Jeff's deployment and trying to give Chesney as much time as possible with her daddy, Liv had tried to get over her hurt by shoving it deep inside. So far, that technique wasn't working especially well.

On the day of his departure, during her early morning time with God, everything felt forced, a matter of soldier-like routine and duty, rather than the intimate warmth and joy Liv had come to experience. To make matters worse, the sibilant hisses of another voice had taken up resident in her head. A voice that encouraged her to encase her heart in icy cold steel. A voice that held more sway at the moment than she cared to admit.

Liv closed her eyes against the frozen hardness in her heart. *Lord, help me get past this without falling apart* Again. She crossed her arms and moved into the living room.

Jeff--clad in his classic blue-tone Navy fatigues and black boots--was minutes away from walking out the front door. Who knew how long it would be before they saw him again...if ever. She pushed the negative thought aside and stepped forward to give him a hug she didn't feel. It was like part of her had frozen over completely. Brief tears stung her eyes, but she quickly brought them under control and took a step back. "Keep us informed as much as possible."

Jeff's face registered profound hurt at her coolness. "You know I will." He hesitated and then cocked his head slightly to the right, his eyes pleading. "Liv, please don't let this come between us. It doesn't have to be this way. I need to know you and I are okay before I leave and face whatever lies ahead."

While his words were true, they were also false. "I understand what you're saying, Jeff. Really I do. And I want to be there for you, but I can't pretend something I don't feel. This is just going to take some time for me to process." Would she ever be able to forgive the Navy and Jeff? And even God? Then, at the last possible minute, her prior deployment experience kicked in. She hugged him once more. "I love you, Jeff. Please come home to us safe and sound." Should she tell him about the baby? Would that make it easier or harder for him to leave?

"Daddy!" Chesney yelled from around the corner and down the hall, followed by the hollow slam of her bedroom door. She rounded the corner, a paper clutched to her chest. She flung herself into Jeff's outstretched arms. "I made you something." She held the paper toward him.

"You did?" He perused the paper, his eyes brightening with tears.

"It says 'I love you' and 'be careful.' Mommy wrote the words out so I could copy them."

He hugged her neck, smiling his appreciation and love to Liv. "I see that. Thank you, baby girl."

A minute later, he set Chesney's feet on the floor and knelt beside her. "You be a good girl for your Mommy, okay?"

Chesney nodded, her eyes already bright with unshed tears. Even at the tender age of four, Chesney had unfortunately learned about the goodbyes that came with having a father in the military. Already she had taken on the stoicism of someone far older.

Jeff stood and pulled Liv into another embrace. "I love you, Liv, and I always will." He whispered the words against her hair, his lips briefly brushing against her ear.

A lump formed in her throat. She battled to find the strength to give him the words of encouragement she knew he sorely needed, but no words would sound.

He released her, sent her one last pleading look, then walked out the door without so much as a second glance.

With the familiar cold freezing her veins to solid ice, Liv quietly shut the door and leaned against it as her sobbing four-year-old crumpled to the floor in utter heartbreak.

To read what happens next . . . follow this link for a copy of the novella and to see what other writing Cathy Bryant has for her followers. . .
PIECES ON EARTH
or **https://cathybryantbooks.wordpress.com/books/pieces-on-earth/**

A Christmas Play

&

A Christmas Skit

"Words satisfy the soul as food satisfies the stomach; the right words on a person's lips brings satisfaction."
Proverbs 18:20 (NLT)

62 ~ THE CHRISTMAS WINDOW

A Play Written by Sandy Jordan

Characters: Frances and Anna sitting on a bench amid bags and boxes.

Hymn: *"Holy, Holy, Holy"*...all four verses...choir

Frances: I find it hard to find this season *holy*. I think all the meaning of Christmas has been lost. I mean how can you feel *holy* in this chaos?

Anna: I don't know. To me it doesn't really matter what's going on around me. I find my peaceful place within and worship Him there. I love the Christmas hymns. I think one of my favorites is *"O Holy Night."*

Frances: I used to love that song. My grandmother used to sing it on Christmas morning and it seemed to set the tone for the day.

Hymn: *"O Holy Night"*

Frances: It's sad things have changed so much. Yet, if you think about it, you hear the Christmas story once a year and it seems to get lost in the volumes written about Christmas. Not the scriptures, but stories about Santa Claus and flying reindeer.

Anna: There is a time and place for everything, but the scriptures bear the greatest meaning for me. The other stories show love and compassion, but the Bible offers us hope, peace and joy. I never tire of reading the Christmas story. I don't regulate it to just Christmas.

Hymn: *"I Love To Tell The Story"*...All 3 verses...choir

Frances: You know, what you say is true, but there is so much suffering going on. There are so many things that aren't right. Miranda's daughter is fifteen and pregnant. Miranda is beside herself. There will be little joy in that house this year.

Anna: Have you ever thought about Mary? Do you think she was prepared to become an unwed mother, acting in supposed sin against her betrothed? Joseph had every right to stone her by the Jewish law.

Frances: Well, we know the baby was God's.

Anna: But the people did not know. They only had the word of a simple village girl. I bet they thought she had cooked up that story to cover her sin. They could have been quick to judge her.

Frances: I have often wondered how Mary felt during all this. I mean, it would be so awesome and so frightening.

(Mary appears on the stage behind them and sits on a bench head bowed as in prayer.

Narrator: Luke 1: 26-38

Hymn First and last verse... *"It Came Upon A Midnight Clear"* ...choir

(A light focuses on Mary on stage)

Frances: She was so willing to obey God, to do His will. That does humble me. I mean, am I that willing to do what God asks of me?

Anna: Remember Mary's song?

Female Narrator: Luke 1:46-55

Hymn *"Mary, Did You Know?"*
Light remains on Mary

Frances: You know women are flexible. A good marriage depends on a woman's ability to compromise. Man, that's an understatement. Anyway, what about Joseph? Do you realize in that country, men were able to kill an unfaithful mate?

Anna: God did not choose just anyone to be Mary's protector and future earthly husband.

Light goes off and Mary leaves the stage....Joseph enters and lies down as if asleep:

Female Narrator: Matthew 1:18-24 *during which angel appears to*

Joseph who sits up. Angel exits. Spotlight: Mary comes to sit on the bench with Joseph beside her

Frances: It was really so simple then. You lived in one town, had a midwife and the birthing system was fairly easy. Today you have the hospitals, the numerous doctors and nurses.

Anna: If you can afford them. The people were as poor then as so many are today. Don't forget they had to pay taxes, too. Poor Mary, she was nearing her due date when they had to go to Bethlehem. I wonder if you could have ridden a donkey for days when you were expecting.

Frances: Wow, you are right. It was a miracle she did not lose the baby or it was born in the middle of the trip. Why the town of Bethlehem?

Hymn: *"O Little Town of Bethlehem"*...1st, 2nd and 4th verses...choir

Male Narrator: Luke 2:1-5

Hymn: *"Oh Come All Ye Faithful"* by choir

Frances: If God was providing for her, protecting her, why was she not provided a nice room and bed for Christ to be born in?

Anna: Christ was born for all people. The blight of homelessness curses our country. Families are being torn apart because they cannot afford their utilities, food, and also provide a good safe home for their children. There is love, but love does not provide the basics. Christ is their hope.

Frances: But a stable?

Female Narrator: Luke 2:6-7

Hymn: *"Away in a Manger"* - Children's choir

Lights go out and Mary and Joseph leave and shepherds come on stage

Frances: There are parts of the story that get to me. I wonder if the shepherds thought that aliens were landing? All those bright lights and angels hovering in the air must have been terrifying.

Anna: Frances, you do have an imagination. No, I think the shepherds knew they were angels. Perhaps like David, the shepherds worshiped God and believed all the promises. Old Testament promises foretold His coming. No, not aliens, but they announced an answer to their prayers.

Angels appear to the shepherds

Hymn: *"Angels We Have Heard on High"*

Male Narrator: Luke 2:8-16

Lights go out. Mary and Joseph come on with the baby. Shepherds join them.

Frances: That's the nativity scene. I used to love those hymns talking about it, but you know, I am sick of hearing mechanical generated versions of "Silent Night." Snow globes, miniature villages, and everything in between.

Anna: I do not agree. My grandmother sang "Silent Night" like an angel. In Germany there was a great deal of poverty. A man wanting to honor God, knowing his church had no working organ or piano, wrote that song for a guitar. It's a simple hymn for a people hungry for hope, for beauty. That song has endured because of its simple beauty.

Hymn: *"Silent Night"* - Choir

Light comes up on nativity scene

Female Narrator: Luke 2:16-20

Hymn: *"Hark The Herald Angels Sing!"*

Choir and angels are singing as they take their place around the manger scene.

Frances: You make it all seem good and gooey. Back then when your grandparents were growing up it was. But now? Stores start Christmas displays before Halloween! Two and a half months of ads, red suited gents with false beards, and those soapy, weepy movies. Give me a break!

Anna: What about the wise men? They traveled a very long way to worship the king, they brought gifts and rehearsed their parts, and they told everyone the joyful news. Frances, this Christmas Window is the chance to spread the gospel...a chance to do good works, to tell a child about Jesus, to share the good news.

Frances: Anna don't you realize the wise men started this materialistic rush to buy, buy, buy?

Anna: Without those first gifts, can you be sure Joseph and Mary and Baby Jesus would have been able to flee to Egypt and survive?

Male narrator: Matthew 2:1-8

Hymn: *"We Three Kings"*
Choir sings first three verses without chorus, then last verse with chorus.... The three kings begin their journey

Female Narrator: Matthew 2: 9-12

Frances: This is okay when the gift helps someone, but what good is a Christmas tree and the fluff and nonsense put onto it? Don't the poor children get disappointed when Santa does not come?

Anna: We all are God's Santa's. We are supposed to see that the poor are as blessed as the rich. The tree represents the living family, the Trinity and eternity with its evergreens. Let's rejoice, sing, and make the most of our Christmas Window!

Frances: I guess you are right, but how many people will really listen, or even care? I am so tired.

Anna: Nonsense, let's start now to spread the word. Everyone, please stand and sing with us *"Joy To The World."*

The End

63 ~ TWO VIEWS OF CHRISTMAS

A Skit Written by Bonnie Clarkson

This is designed for church use, not as a family skit. The advantage for a church is that it is short enough to leave time for choir songs or other things a church does for Christmas. It also is short enough that people can be get home for family gatherings. It ends with a pastor or designated person giving the salvation message. I left it that way for the church to say exactly how their church wants to present the gospel and to give the church a chance to make a personal call to join their church.

Setting: Nursing home, modern day

Props: 2 wheelchairs, small table, an artificial, tabletop Christmas tree

Characters:

> **GEORGE**: confined to wheelchair, Christian
>
> **RANDY:** confined to wheelchair, non-Christian
>
> **SANTA CLAUS** sponsored by Chamber of Commerce
>
> **SECULAR CAROLERS**
>
> **CHRISTIAN CAROLERS**
>
> **SMALL CHILD:** 6-year-old or less, girl
>
> **NURSING HOME STAFF**

SECULAR CAROLERS: (Sing *"Jingle Bells"* and *"Deck the Halls"* and leave.)

RANDY: Well, *there's* something to enjoy—those songs. What a terrible time to be in a nursing home! Christmas time! That tree *(pointing to table-top tree)* is as ugly as my mood!

GEORGE: You think that tree is ugly? I was thinking how thoughtful of

189

someone to put in a tree to remind me of Christmases past. I was remembering playing with my cousins. And the food and smell of coffee remind me of . . .

CHRISTIAN CAROLERS: (Sing *"Silent Night," "We Three Kings," and "Joy to the World"* and leave.)

GEORGE: Those old songs are so *wonderful*! They speak to me as much now as they did years ago.

RANDY: Speak to you? They didn't do *anything* for me.

GEORGE: Oh yes, they spoke to me. Not like *"Jingle Bells"* and *"Deck the Halls." "Silent Night," "We Three Kings,"* and *"Joy to the World"* speak to me about the hope I have as a Christian.

RANDY: What hope?

GEORGE: *(Slowly, with emphasis)* The hope of becoming a better person. The hope of seeing loved ones again. The hope of not dying alone.

RANDY: *(Grunts and looks away.)*

SANTA CLAUS: Ho! Ho! Ho! Merry Christmas. Just bringing a gift from the Chamber of Commerce. *(**RANDY** takes the gift.)*

GEORGE: *(Looks at gift and hands it back.)*

SANTA CLAUS: *(Confused)* You don't want it?

GEORGE: No. Save it for someone who really needs it. But let me give you a gift. It's John 3:16 (KJV). "For God so loved the world, that He gave His only begotten Son that whosoever believeth in Him should not perish, but have everlasting life." You'll never use up that gift.

SANTA CLAUS: *(Unsure.)* Yeah. Sure. Goodbye.

RANDY: Shame on you for not accepting his gift! How do you think that made him feel!

GEORGE: I don't suppose he'll feel anything but a little loss in his pocketbook. They were just coupons. *(Sadly)* I am so tired of Christmas being used to make money.

SMALL CHILD: *(Crying at the door.)*

GEORGE: What's wrong, little girl? Why are you crying? Are you lost? *(Girl nods.)* That's a lonely feeling, being lost, isn't it? *(Girl nods again, still crying.)* I can't get up to help you, but if you come here, I'll hold your hand. *(Girl walks over to him, holds his hand and gradually stops crying.)*

NURSE: *(Enters and addresses **SMALL CHILD**.)* There you are. Your mother was getting worried about you. *(Both leave.)*

RANDY: *(Impressed)* I can't believe how just holding her hand was enough to stop her crying.

GEORGE: I knew what she needed because that's how my Father in Heaven treats me. Did you know that the Bible says we must be like children to enter the Kingdom of God? When I chose Jesus, I accepted His authority and trusted— *(Starts gasping for breath and convulsing.)*

RANDY: *(Hollers at passing **NURSE**)* Nurse! I need help in here for George!

NURSE: *(One look at **GEORGE** and calls for **STAFF**)* Let's get him moved STAT! *(Takes **GEORGE** out of room)*

RANDY: *(Looks where George had been, long silence)* I wonder what he meant by *choosing* Jesus.

PASTOR OR DESIGNATED PERSON USES STORY TO TIE CHRISTMAS INTO THE SALVATION PLAN.

Let There Be Music

"I will sing of Thy steadfast love, O Lord, forever;
with my mouth I will proclaim Thy faithfulness
to all generations."
Psalm 89:1 (RSV)

64 ~ ANGELS WE HAVE HEARD ON HIGH

ANONYMOUS - ON PURPOSE

If you have heard professional or very polished choirs lifting their lilting voices, or lifted your own, to sing this old Christmas carol, you know how readily we associate it with Christmas. You can't sing the song and mope. It is a song of joy, of exuberance, though, the writer claims, the proclamation of Jesus' arrival in Bethlehem was sung sweetly to those startled sheep watchers. And maybe so.

After all, perhaps most shepherds expected a quiet night watching over their flock. Tradition tells us those sheep lived to die as sacrifices for a human's sins on a bloody altar. That first Christmas night, perhaps the shepherds judged just how close that distant howl was. Maybe they sized up the critter eager for lamb chops as its midnight feast. The shepherds were armed and ready to protect what was theirs.

And then, to the lowest rung on the socio-economic ladder, a heaven-sent messenger incites their fears, tells them to remain calm, and declares they have been chosen to hear the most amazing news this world would ever hear. These who kept the sacrificial lambs in good shape, without spot or blemish, now begin to learn that the Holy Sacrificial Lamb of God, the Last Sacrifice, has come to earth. Their minds may not have fully grasped it yet, but just maybe a few began to understand that the Precious Lamb of God would someday be slain for the sins of the shepherds, the kings, and the lot of mankind in between. So, listen, meditatively, to the song's echoing words:

Angels we have heard on high
Sweetly singing o'er the plain
And the mountains in reply
Echoing their joyous strains
Gloria, in excelsis Deo!
Gloria, in excelsis Deo!
Shepherds, why this jubilee?
Why your joyous strains prolong?
What the gladsome tidings be

Which inspire your heavenly songs? ....Gloria
Come to Bethlehem and see
Christ Whose birth the angels sing;
Come, adore on bended knee,
Christ, the Lord, the newborn King.....Gloria
See Him in a manger laid,
Jesus, Lord of heaven and earth;
Mary, Joseph, lend your aid,
With us sing our Savior's birth. .....Gloria

I think the song's writer studied the scriptures before composing the words and music. Because I sometimes read scripture, meditate upon it, and then write, occasionally poetically, what I pray others consider helpful, I used the Internet to do research behind this Christmas song.

Interestingly, in about 1862, we're told, Bishop James Chadwick penned "Angels We Have Heard on High." Apparently he didn't just have a burst of inspiration and create this song. Wikipedia and a United Methodist Church's Discipleship website indicate Chadwick relied heavily upon both the French carol *"Les Anges dans nos campagnes /Angels in our countryside"* composition and lyrics which appeared in hymnals as early as 1819. That composer/poet is unknown. If we go to the Christmas account in the book of Luke, we read about the angels announcing the birth of Jesus Christ, the Savior, to the shepherds.

Announcing the birth of the Son of God to shepherds reminds us that God and His angels show no favouritism, no prejudice. The angels not only proclaimed the Birth, but also invited the shepherds to be the first outsiders to go to Bethlehem and find the newborn babe wrapped in swaddling clothes and lying in a manger. Perhaps those sometimes invisible beings witnessed or somehow knew the exact details about the Savior's arrival: Bethlehem, newborn, swaddling cloths, manger.

Don't you find it encouraging that the shepherds didn't delay? Not, "Let's wait til morning," or "Let's go find some learned theologian who can verify that we heard right or have the right to go." God sent angels to them because their hearts would respond to Truth. Off they went.

Can't you almost smell the stable as it temporarily warmed the chilled herdsmen? I've been in livestock barns and sheep sheds, even at night a few times. I've birthed children, so it's easy for me to imagine the encounter. A newborn, hair still damp, snuggly wrapped, and bedded down within the protective manger. Yes, there He was: God's Son had

194

come to earth on a mission. "Savior" was God's word for Him on a few occasions before His birth. Could any in the party, including Mary and Joseph, see the Newborn and realize how costly His coming would be?

But after the quiet whispers and the conversation that confirmed to Mary and her espoused husband that God wasn't keeping Jesus a secret, the shepherds left "praising God" and establishing the simplest template for missions: Encounter Christ, praise God He graciously let you do that, then tell others the Savior has come to take away the sins of the world.

Perhaps there are two considerations for us as we go through this Christmas season. Think about the fact that the original writer/composer is unknown. If your church uses hymnals or posts the author along with the copyright notice, several hymns' writers are "Anonymous." Many times I've been moved by that fact. God uses someone's work without that person getting noticed or praised – in human terms.

So, question one: Would we be willing to leave our name off our work or let others take credit for it in the years to come, simply because we trust God to use something we wrote or did? Perhaps in heaven God has planned a grand parade of the "Anonymouses" and we'll be able to give credit where credit is due; but meantime, for us, are we willing to do something wonderful for the Lord without anyone knowing we did it? Please understand, however, I'm not opposed to giving and receiving credit for work completed because here on earth, compensation is part of the system that keeps us from becoming beggars. Sometimes, though, maybe we need to discover the joy of anonymity.

The second question for us as our voices travel up and down the scale singing a syllable or two of "Glor-i-a," might be, "Do we keep the Good News of Jesus's birth, life, death on the cross for our sins, resurrection, and ascension a secret? Or do we spread the Good News, just as the shepherds did?"

PRAYER:

Father God, thank You so much for loving us more than enough to send Your Holy Son to become the Lamb that takes away my sins and the sins of the world. Father, please help me humbly serve You first and foremost. I need Your help when I share Truth with those who need to hear it. May my life bring You honor and glory even before I arrive to bring You glory in Your presence. In Jesus' Name and for His Sake, Amen.

65 ~ LET ALL MORTAL FLESH KEEP SILENCE

JEANETTA CHRYSTIE

John 6:38 "I have come down from heaven ... to do the will of Him who sent me." (NASB)

Watching the Raleigh Ringers handbell choir is a delight. *(You can watch them at www.rr.org/Multimedia/Video-Gallery or YouTube.com to see samples.)* In listening to their concert, I recently rediscovered a Christmas carol: "Let All Mortal Flesh Keep Silent".

This Christmas carol describes who Christ is and why He left Heaven to come to Earth. The words are from the fourth century liturgy of St. James, which is still chanted by Orthodox Christians in Jerusalem on the Sunday after Christmas. It invites us to wonder at the mystery of Christ's incarnation as described in Isaiah 6, John 6:35-58 and Revelation 4:8.

Its melody is from a seventeenth century French song. The words and tune were combined as a Christmas carol in 1906 by English composer Ralph Vaughan Williams. While it isn't a carol that is often sung around the fireplace, nor is it well-known to children, it is a beautiful piece with words of prophecy and wonder.

> Let all mortal flesh keep silence,
> And with fear and trembling stand;
> Ponder nothing earthly minded,
> For with blessing in His hand,
> Christ our God to earth descendeth
> Our full homage to demand.
>
> King of kings, yet born of Mary,
> As of old on earth He stood,
> Lord of lords, in human vesture,

In the body and the blood;
He will give to all the faithful
His own self for heavenly food.

Rank on rank the host of heaven
Spreads its vanguard on the way,
As the Light of light descendeth
From the realms of endless day,
That the powers of hell may vanish
As the darkness clears away.

At His feet the six winged seraph,
Cherubim with sleepless eye,
Veil their faces to the presence,
As with ceaseless voice they cry:
Alleluia, Alleluia, Alleluia,
Lord Most High!

PRAYER:

*Dear Lord and Savior, Thank you for Your sacrifice, for Your
indescribable gift and our ransom. May we, this Christmas, lift our
voices with Your angels in praise. Amen.*

66 ~ I HEARD THE BELLS ON CHRISTMAS DAY

JEANETTA CHRYSTIE

Psalm 30:11 "You turned my wailing into dancing..." (NIV)

When I think of Christmas music, I think of harps and handbells. One of my favorite harpists is Greg Buchanan,* probably because I heard him several years ago at our Seattle-area church. During the concert he played many familiar Christmas carols, briefly telling a story behind the creation of each carol.

I listened and began taking notes about the history of several of my favorite Christmas carols, of which I have many: *Silent Night, Angels We Have Heard On High, It Came Upon A Midnight Clear, Joy to the World, O Come All Ye Faithful, O Little Town of Bethlehem,* and several others.

Christmas can be a difficult time for people experiencing trials.

The story that remains most firmly in my memory is the story of *I Heard the Bells on Christmas Day* because out of tragedy came beauty; from loss came hope.

American poet Henry Wadsworth Longfellow wrote the words on December 25, 1864. Three years earlier, his wife Fanny had died from severe burns suffered in a freak accident. He grieved every Christmas without her. Now, his son Charles lay before him seriously injured from Civil War wounds. Longfellow despaired of hope and wrote "there is no peace on Earth."

On Christmas morning, he heard bells ringing from nearby churches. He looked up toward Heaven and prayed. His hope and faith were restored despite tragedies and he completed the poem we now know as *I Heard the Bells on Christmas Day.*

Although originally titled *Christmas Bells* with seven stanzas, two were removed in 1872 by John Baptiste Calkin because they referred to the

U.S. Civil War. Baptiste rearranged the poem a little and added a cheerful tune to create the Christmas carol we know as *I Heard the Bells on Christmas Day.*

Every time I sing or hear this carol, I pray for those who struggle to celebrate Christmas.

PRAYER:

Dear Heavenly Father, Thank you for our blessings. Help us remember those who hurt most during this season of the year. Amen.

* Listen to the harpist through this link: (http://gregbuchananministries.org/music_demos.html)

67 ~ AWAY IN A MANGER

JEANETTA CHRYSTIE

Luke 2:7 "She wrapped Him in cloths and placed Him in a manger..."
(NIV)

Aunt Carol. At least that's what I grew up calling her. Years later I learned she is my Dad's cousin. When I was 6 years old, she was "Aunt" Carol, and my first piano teacher.

The first full song she taught me was *Away In A Manger*. It begins with an almost descending scale, and she used it to help me learn to read musical notes and cross over my fingers to play it correctly. I'm glad there were few witnesses to my stumbling practicing on the fellowship hall's piano at First Baptist Church of Carl Junction. Each time I played it correctly earned a big smile and words of praise from Aunt Carol.

Away In A Manger was one of my childhood's favorite Christmas carols, perhaps because it was one of the first songs I learned to play. But also I was fascinated by the tender message of Baby Jesus, tucked snugly into a manger with Mary and Joseph and farm animals gathered around Him. When combined with the simple *Cradle Song* melody composed by William James Kirkpatrick, it created sweet images in my mind.

Early hymn publications attributed *Away In A Manger* to Martin Luther, saying he wrote it for his children, and called it *Luther's Cradle Hymn*. However, modern research discounts Luther as the author. Also, the third verse was added in the early 1900s by John T. McFarland, a Methodist minister.

Unlike my "Aunt" Carol, I never became an outstanding pianist; however, I continue to enjoy learning. The attention to detail that Carol taught me has carried over into other areas of my life.

Carol Gaddy Conner has traveled to play concerts, recorded albums, and composed many hymn arrangements and medleys. Let me invite you to experience her medley of *For the Beauty of the Earth* with *This is My Father's World* (at https://www.youtube.com/watch?v=ygnSBuB74zs) or you can simply search on YouTube for "*My Father's World* by Carol Gaddy Conner". Her photography illustrating her arrangement of this medley is a lovely interpretation of the message of both songs.

Meanwhile, I probably need to begin practicing on the old Lowrey organ I inherited so I can play *Away in the Manger* well enough this Christmas for family to be able to sing along.

PRAYER:

Dear Father God, Thank you for endowing so many of your children with talents that enrich our lives. May we each focus on You this Christmas season and share generously of our blessings with others. In Jesus' name we pray, Amen.

Editor's Note: Perhaps you will enjoy another rendition of "Away in a Manger" - ***https://www.youtube.com/watch?v=4l05A4c0bZA***

68 ~ THOUGHTS ON "MARY, DID YOU KNOW?"

JEANETTA CHRYSTIE

Luke 2:7 "And she gave birth to her first-born son; and wrapped Him in cloths…" NASB

One of our favorite Christmas songs is *Mary, Did You Know?* which we first heard on our Seattle-area Christian radio station. My husband, Keith, sang it in our church with a young lady from among the church's youth group dressed as Mary and holding a baby doll wrapped as Baby Jesus. As *Mary* cradled *Baby Jesus*, a piano played softly and *Mary* pretended to coo and giggle with her baby.

Then the words began, coming from behind *Mary* as Keith slowly walked closer. "Mary did you know that your baby boy will one day walk on water…" People watched with rapt attention as the young *Mary* continued to act as though she were interacting with her baby. Mark Lowry's lyrics continued, "…Did you know that your baby boy has walked where angels trod?" and the sanctuary was perfectly quiet.

The next phrase, "And when you kiss your little baby, you've kissed the face of God" seemed to bring a collective gasp as the import of that line touched everyone's emotions. The song continued, with Buddy Greene's sweetly haunting melody drifting through the sanctuary.

I watched the emotion on Keith and *Mary's* faces; then looked around at others who had tears in their eyes as the reality of that original manger scene became so real to everyone. The final line proclaimed, *"This sleeping child you're holding is the great I AM"* and seemed to charge the air with expectation. Few Christmas songs have ever touched my heart as deeply as this one, perhaps partly due to the deeply meaningful shared experience of feeling that first Christmas in our hearts.

My favorite version of this song is still Mark Lowry's on YouTube* with the Gaither Vocal Band. If you need help to focus on Jesus this Christmas, find and listen to this song.

PRAYER:

Dear Heavenly Father, Thank You for giving your Son for us. His love is our true hope and joy, and our only path to peace. Help us focus on Christ in our Christmas. In Jesus' Name, Amen.

* Listen and watch Mark Lowry sing this song on YouTube: https://www.youtube.com/watch?v=kpFCbJpm5Zk

69 ~ MOHR SANG TENOR, GRUBER SANG BASS

MARGERY KISBY WARDER

In Oberndorf, Austria, it was Christmas Eve. Father Joseph Mohr had decisions to make. The organ, vital to the village's worship service, would not play. Mohr was a pastor and a musician, but he was not an organ rebuilder. Without the organ, the choir would have no accompaniment. Without music, it just wouldn't be a Christmas Eve service.

What options did young Father Mohr have?

Mohr could pass the word through the riverside village in 1818 and cancel services. Most likely his congregation would focus their disappointment on the malfunctioning organ and not on their pastor who had been in their midst but a year.

If Mohr asked the choir to sing acappella, but without more time to prepare, would their efforts leave people less than blessed?

Father Mohr had a third option, but that option was riskiest of all. When he chose it, he had no way of knowing thousands of future Christmas Eves would seem incomplete without singing the song first sung that Christmas Eve in Oberndorf. Generation upon generation is grateful Mohr chose to risk much to proclaim Christmas truths that night now so long ago.

Dare I propose that Christmas began, after all, when God took a very great risk?

In heaven, even in eternity past, the Godhead - the Father, the Son, and the Holy Ghost - were, as always, in perfect harmony as One. Millennia before Mohr's dilemma, God pledged to initiate a rescue of us, His loved ones. Why? Because we humans earn damnation when we leave God out of our lives. God's chosen people, too, in the Old Testament times, had turned away to worship handmade gods and follow inborn desires. His people, like we who choose to sin, and every sin is a choice, willingly subjected themselves to bondage, the price disobedience extracts. Whimpers and pleas rose to God's ear. Each as a plea reminded God of His promise to be faithful, to send a Redeemer, to send One who could rescue us from the consequences of our sinful nature.

Of course God had not forgotten. God had waited for exactly the right time.

Right time? For whom? Perhaps for God's people, the Israelites, a Redeemer couldn't arrive at a better time. They'd lost their land. Rome treated them harshly. One of their own sat on the throne in Jerusalem, but his jealous heart had no intention of acknowledging God's Promised One. Enemies mocked the religion of the Jewish people, wherever devout Jews still practiced their faith. Life's worth depended upon the whim of a ruler, and it appeared God's chosen people were again at risk of being wiped off the face of the earth. Or, was also the right time when crucifixion would be a method for punishing threats to order? Hmm.

So, on a quiet night of long ago, God risked His Son to keep a promise.

On that night in overcrowded Bethlehem, God risked giving His helpless but Holy, Son through birth to a timid, inexperienced maiden from Nazareth. That was a risk.

Again God risked the rescue of mankind when He chose Joseph as the guardian father-in-waiting. Joseph was good, but he was a peasant carpenter. Just months earlier, he quietly tried to get out of his commitment to marry the maiden, Mary, who had returned from a visit to her cousin. She explained her body's changes by assuring Joseph she had never been with a man. Joseph needed God to convince him that Mary spoke the truth.

Yes, God took many risks that very first Christmas when Jesus came as an infant whose ministry would not be fully known for decades, and then most would resist the love and truth He offered.

Father Mohr knew many Christmas truths but sometimes truth doesn't relieve the uneasiness accompanying risk-taking. Still, what did he have to lose?

Mohr's unusual idea might bring ridicule; his offered might be rejected.

He might fail, especially since the calendar said it was Christmas Eve.

He would need help, but friends might refuse to help.

If he moved the plan forward but a disgruntled congregation reported him, would he be moved to another congregation with a reputation to live down?

Mohr had studied music. He could play the violin. But churches relied upon organ music for their services. Lately, he'd played a guitar. Guitars did not hold a candle to an organ for sacred music, but since the church's organ was not an option for Christmas Eve in his village church, perhaps they'd tolerate the guitar if he could accompany a song. Which song?

Two years earlier, in 1816, Joseph Mohr had studied the Biblical story about Jesus's birth and wrote a rhyme to retell it. That poem was in his drawer. Mohr would need a melody for his little set of verses:

> Silent night, holy night, all is calm, all is bright,
> Round yon virgin mother and child, Holy infant so tender and mild
> Sleep in heavenly peace, Sleep in heavenly peace.

> Silent night, holy night, Shepherds quake at the sight;
> Glories stream from heaven afar, Heavenly hosts sing, "Alleluia!"
> Christ the Savior is born, Christ the Savior is born.

Silent night, holy night. Son of God, Love's pure light;
Radiant beams from Thy holy face
With the dawn of redeeming grace,
Jesus, Lord, at Thy birth, Jesus, Lord, at Thy birth.

Father Mohr trudged over to Franz Gruber's busy household. He took the risk of showing Gruber his poem. Gruber was struck with the simplicity of the message and the appropriateness of it for their Christmas Eve service. With little effort, the church's organist created a tune and Mohr picked it out on his guitar. No, it was not as awe-inspiring as Handel's Messiah that had drawn audiences for three-quarters of a century, but with simplicity Mohr's rhyme retold the Savior's birth, too.

All of that was commendable, but could the choir learn the song in just a short practice? That Christmas Eve, the choir sang the chorus while Mohr played the tune on his guitar. The two men's voices carried the new tune on the verses; Mohr sang tenor and Gruber sang bass. When the service ended, the poem, destined to become a Christmas favorite around the world, was left on the silent organ.

Sometime after Christmas, the repairman came to rebuild the organ and read the poem. He began making the poem a public phenomenon.

Mohr never expected to gain fame or fortune from the solution he strummed on his guitar that Christmas Eve; he died penniless and unaware his poem had become popular.

Gruber was contacted after the King of Prussia ordered the authors of the popular "Silent Night" be properly identified.

One hundred years after that Christmas Eve in 1818, its melody silenced the guns of war as one side, then the other, sang the words in their own tongue. Few songs can do that.

If you want to spend an evening listening to "Silent Night, Holy Night" this Christmas season, you can search online and hear it in most languages. While you prayerfully listen to the song or the scriptures declaring that a loving God risked all to let you know He came to rescue you, ask yourself if you've tucked something away in a "drawer" that God might want you to turn over to Him so God can bless it. Why do you think God entrusted you with it?

God is the instigator of creativity. If God has blessed you or me with a skill, a song, a poem, a story, or the ability to send a kind word that might change a heart, or maybe even a world, what's keeping us from sharing that gift this Christmas? What we offer Him might make a world of difference to someone else, far beyond what we can imagine. What will you risk to be faithful to the Lord?

PRAYER:
Father God and Lord Jesus, Thank You for prompting us to learn more about You so we can demonstrate our love for You more thoroughly. Thank You that You were present at creation and You placed within us the desire to be creative and useful. Lord, if we are sitting too long on work You called us to do, embolden us to be about what matters most to You. In Jesus' Holy Name, Amen.

Poetry

"Let no unwholesome word proceed from your mouth but only such a word as is good for edification according to the need of the moment, so that it will give grace to those who hear."

(Ephesians 4:29 NASB)

70 ~ WRITE A CHRISTMAS POEM

JANE LANDRETH

Have you ever wanted to be a poet? Some kinds of poetry do not require words that rhyme. You can write poems like these even if you have never written a poem before. Try writing a Christmas poem.

One kind of poetry that does not have to rhyme is called **cinquain** (SIN-kane). Here is the way to write it:

1. Word—title
2. Words—explain title
3. Words—express a feeling about the title
4. Words—express an action about the title
1 Word—means the same as the title

Here is an example of a **cinquain** using the subject--Jesus:

Jesus
God's Son
Jesus loves me.
Let us worship Him.
Lord

Now you choose a subject. A Christmas subject might be from the Bible, a Biblical character, a Bible custom, a truth or an idea. The title might just be Christmas or love. Write a **cinquain** on the subject you choose with the formula given. Remember, the poem does not have to rhyme.

Use the same subject or pick another subject and write a **haiku** (HI-koo). This is a form of Japanese poetry. It does not need to rhyme either.

Here is the way to write it:

Line 1—word or words with a total of five syllables.
Line 2—word or words with a total of seven syllables.
Line 3—word or words with a total of five syllables.

Here is an example of this type of poetry:

God sent a Savior
To be born in a manger.
Mary, the mother.

Now try writing a Christmas poem. See how much fun writing can be!

71 ~ CHRISTMAS CARD BLESSING

MARILYN BOONE

It's time to mail the cards again,
I heard the calendar speak.
Alarmed, I ran to check the date,
How was Christmas in one week?

Just seven days were all I had,
To send a season's greeting,
I raced to find my address book,
For time was ever fleeting.

I started with the letter A,
As urgency flowed through me,
That was until I saw the name,
Of my sweet Grandpa Rudy.

I paused as I remembered him,
Only months since I had cried,
Wishing heaven had an address,
Since his no longer applied.

The hurried feeling slowed its pace,
With each new page I turned,
Scribbles and lines for old and new,
For a past I sometimes yearned.

With wistful thought I closed the book,
Rarely opened anymore,
Unlike the modern contact list,
One's life journey it does store.

Its alphabet of memories,

Of my friends and closest kin,
Evoked a quiet prayer of thanks,
For the blessings that had been.

I placed a stamp upon each card,
No more panic, only cheer,
A heart now filled with gratitude,
Knowing Christmas Day was near.

72 ~ CONTINUUM

SANDY JORDAN

Softly glowing innocence
radiating out of childish faces,
yellow tinsel halos on golden curls,
awkward wings flutter
on bed sheet robes,
tiny feet in white socks peek out
pointing this way and that
as they fight the urge to squirm
on this holy night
celebrating the birth of Jesus
a baby in a manger
that they are singing about in lisp,
between missing front teeth
bringing tears to the eyes of the saints
growing close to their homecoming day
the church will go on,
the continuum has taken the stage
the future is assured
in these tiny angels
singing with all their hearts,
loving Jesus
on this holy Christmas night.

73 ~ CHRISTMAS IN ARIZONA

SOFI MCCUTCHEON

Tastes like donuts with chocolate sprinkles, peppermint ice cream, and fish tacos
Smells like warm waffles, baked apples, and maple syrup
Looks like Christmas lights, silver bows, and colorful wrapping paper
Sounds like bells ringing, Grandma's carols on the piano, and packages opening
Feels like nice hugs, crisp dollar bills, and a soft cuddly bear

74 ~ CAROLING

MARGERY KISBY WARDER

I sang for "them" ~
The elderly,
The lonely.
The shut-in.
And days closed
One year
After another.
Now, all too soon,
The carolers come
and
sing
to me.

75 ~ THE GREATEST GIFT OF ALL

T.R. HOBBS-YORK

Under the tree sits gifts of all kinds.
Some are theirs. Some are mine.
The tree is covered with tinsel and balls.
The house is decorated from wall to wall.
On the stereo sits Santa and spouse.
"Will he and his reindeer visit our house?"
Over the fireplace "Merry Christmas" is hung.
On the stereo "Merry Christmas" is sung.
I look around and my eyes suddenly see
a group on the stand that are calling to me.
Alone that small group reverently stands;
Mary and Joseph and the three Wise Men;
A shepherd boy and some sheep watch nearby
as an Angel of God peers down from the sky.
In the center of it all a boy child lay
sweetly resting in a manger of hay.
Jesus of Nazareth is the man-child's name;
Sent down from God – His gift to man.
The child that lay sleeping upon the sweet hay
would be man's salvation in a short-distant day.
But on this – the day of His birth
there was a sweet peace covering the earth.
Every man from commoner to king
felt the peace the child was to bring.
I look down on the group as it silently stands
and I'm thankful to God for His gift to man.
Humbly I realize in the heart of it all
Jesus Christ is the Greatest Gift of All.

76 ~ ONLY ONES

BONNIE CLARKSON

At the Savior's birth we are told
He was worshipped by shepherds at least.
Later He received frankincense, myrrh, and gold
From wise men from way back east.

But why were they the only ones?
Where were the experts who knew what God foretold?
Did God tell any priest of His Son?
How many wives wanted to go, but husbands did withhold?

Did someone have to go see their land?
Did another rather tend his cows?
Had a man in marriage just taken his wife's hand?
Is that why they could not go just now?

We are not told of those who would not mind
The call to come enjoy God's deed.
All we know is that none is so deaf and blind
As those who will not hear and see.

77 ~ MARY'S PONDERINGS

MARGERY KISBY WARDER

O Little Babe, asleep upon the stable's hay,
What kind of love makes You come to us this way?
What kind of love took You from Your heavenly home
And placed You here where You'll oft be alone?
O Little Babe, You smile at me,
As though You see things I cannot see.

O Young Child, You run, You play –
And yet, I know You see life in a different way.
When other children grab, You give –
Tell me, Young Child, who's teaching You how to live?
O Young Child, You smile at me,
As though You see things I cannot see.

My Fine Young Man, why must You go away?
We've built our home, hoping You'd stay.
Needs out there? Why, there're needs here, too.
What is it, Young Man, that beckons You?
O Young Man, You smile at me,
As though You see things I cannot see.

O Dying Son, hanging upon that cruel cross,
Can You know how much I feel this loss?
I hurt for You – and for me – this is so unjust!
Can You mean, even still, I simply trust?
O Dying Son, You smile – even now – at me,
As though You see things I cannot see.

Hallelujah! My Risen Lord! My Savior and My God!
I'd hoped death's tomb was not the end!
I now see: Your life, Your death, was for all men.
'What kind of love brought You from heav'n above?'
Ah, I see, My Risen Lord – I see 'twas Calvary Love!

78 ~ CHRISTMAS MEMORIES

ASTRID KISBY

REPRINTED BY PERMISSION FROM "ASTRID'S GIFT TO HER LOVED ONES"

A season is quickly approaching,
A time of reflections and cheer
As loved ones, friends, and relation,
Surround us from there and here.

We recall in our endless hustle
The days of our younger years
A delight was the country school program
Santa's visit provided much cheer.

My very first doll was discovered
At the top of a Christmas tree,
Her body of cloth-covered sawdust,
And lettered with "ABC's."

Her head was of beautiful china,
Her eyes, a heavenly blue,
Her hair, jet black and in fashion,
Her cheeks, a delicate hue.

Our home was filled with excitement
As we entered each day after school,

The oven still warm from much baking,
The wood box near empty of fuel.

Our mother kept faithfully busy
For all in the house must be clean,
Awaiting this sacred occasion
When nothing astray should be seen.

Our church with its stained arched windows,
Stands out in our memories dear,
Of long ago glad celebrations
Tho' there could be moments of fear.

My piece, did I know, could I say it,
When the turn became mine to declare
The wonderful story of Jesus
The people were waiting to share?

Now these are some times I remember
And others I fail to recall,
For I have passed many a Christmas
Yet, somehow, have loved them all.

Editor's note: "Astrid's Gift to Her Loved Ones" contains more than 100 original poems and is available online.

79 ~ MARY'S REFLECTIONS

Poems from
"From the Cradle to the Cross: God's Promise Fulfilled"

T. R. HOBBS-YORK

Hello, Little One!
I'm so glad you are here.
I touch Your sweet face
so precious and dear.
We've waited so long
to see God's Holy Son.
I've waited so long
to hold You, precious One.
I stroke tiny shoulders that will
bear the weight of the world.
I look into eyes that know every
woman, man, boy and girl.
I touch tiny fingers that will
reach out to the lost.
I hold this dear body that will
know the pain of the cross.
This one innocent life will
be convicted of no crime.
This one gentle heart will
bear all sin for mankind.
Sweet, tender boy You will
become a kind, gentle man
Spreading Your Father's Word
throughout all of His land.
Sweet, gentle Spirit, You are
God's Son and delight.
You will be a safe harbor
from the storms of this life.

You will be healer and teacher,
Shepherd and Lamb;
The solid Rock and Foundation
on which we will stand.
Looking now into the depths
of Your kind, gentle eyes
It is hard to believe that You
will one day be despised.
You are so tiny and helpless
that it is hard to believe
That resting upon Your shoulders
is this world's reprieve.
Tomorrow You will bear the
weight of the sins of mankind.
But today, my dear son, You
you are Joseph's and mine.
We will guide You, protect You,
and raise You with love,
With the knowledge that You
are God's Son from above.
We will guard You with devotion
until Your time is at hand
To do Your Father's bidding
and begin His great Plan.
I thank God in Heaven for
giving You into our care.
May we do justice to His trust;
This is our prayer.

80 ~ THE FORGOTTEN FATHER

T. R. HOBBS-YORK

When we take the time to contemplate
the birth of God's own Son
We forget about and overlook
a very special man.
We honor Jesus' mother calling
her blessed among women.
This is good and right. But there is
another we have forgotten.
He was a very special man
and a carpenter by trade.
A kind and gentle man who
also did as God had bade.
When an angel came to Him
and told him Mary was with child;
How must he have felt? Angry? Hurt?
Did he feel she was defiled?
It could not have been easy accepting
Mary would have another's baby.
For at that time an unwed mother was
considered anything but a lady.
But Joseph did not put her aside
as another would have done.
He took her for his bride even though
they probably were shunned.
He stood fast and resolute
and firm by her side.
He held firm to his promise
To claim Mary as his bride.
He did as God commanded
And took Mary into his home.
And he claimed the baby Jesus
And raised him as his own.
He taught him all he knew

In his kind and gentle way.
When Jesus took a fall,
Joseph soothed his pain away.
He raised him with love, with heart
And warmth and pride.
He was a father and a friend,
A teacher and a guide.
Joseph did not shirk his duty;
He did not disobey God's command.
He raised the baby Jesus with
A tender, guiding hand.
How God must have trusted Joseph
When He put Jesus in his care.
What a special man he must have been;
Good, honest, trustworthy, and fair.
How God must have loved Joseph
For raising His only Son.
It speaks well of this simple man
Who did not say "no" or run.
It is understandable that Mary is
Considered "blessed" among women.
But consider the carpenter Joseph
Who also obeyed God's command.
Of all of the step-fathers who have passed
Down through the sands of time
Can any be more special than the
Carpenter who was good and kind?
The step-father who took a backseat
And did not interfere.
The man who soothed God's brow
And wiped away his tears.
What a wonderful man, the carpenter,
Joseph must have been
To accept the immense burden of
Raising Jesus from babe to man.
To provide, protect and care for
God's Son without complaint.

He shouldered this awesome burden
And did not stumble or faint.
And the most amazing thing that
Stands out in my mind
Is that Joseph is seldom mentioned.
He's been forgotten down through time.
But I know God has not forgotten
The man who raised His Son.
He has not over-looked all that
The carpenter, Joseph, had done.
Though we are feeble-minded and
Have not given Joseph his due
God has not forgotten Joseph's obedience.
He will reward this too.
If there is any man in history
Who deserves respect and praise
It is the gentle Joseph, who took
Jesus as his own to raise.

81 ~ A STAR LED THE WAY

T. R. HOBBS-YORK

There on the mantle
The Christ Child lay.
A manger for His bed
And a pillow of hay.
Mary, His mother,
Sits quietly by his side
As Joseph stands guard
Over God's SON and pride.
Overhead, shining as
Bright as the sun
The STAR which led Wise Men
To God's Holy One
Is shining down gently
Showing THE WAY
To sinners and saints
Who want to be saved.
It beckons us onward
Toward God's Holy Light
Who promises forgiveness,
Peace and respite.
To the weak He gives strength.
To the weary He gives rest.
To the frightened – courage.
To the dying – new breath.
To the hurting He gives solace.
To the angry – release.
To the sorrowful – joy.

To the prisoner – reprieve.
To the confused He gives guidance.
To the lost – new direction.
To the homeless – a home.
To the imperfect – perfection.
To the addict release
From torment and pain.
To the persecuted – justice; and
Sinners cleansed from sins' stain.
Satan's arrows on earth
He captures and binds
Giving all a new world
More loving and kind.
In those two tiny hands
And shoulders so strong;
In that one gentle heart
Is forgiveness of all wrongs.
There in that cradle
Lay God in man's form.
His blood for our sins.
Our Shelter from storms.
One small life for many.
One heart reaches out
To love us in spite of
Our questions and doubt.
In the shadowy darkness
A star led the way
To the Savior of mankind
At rest on the hay.

A SMALL COLLECTION OF POEMS

PEARL PIERSON

(Reprinted by permission from "Found A Life of Christ")

82 ~ I

"Fear not: for, behold, I bring you good tidings of great joy, which shall be to all people. For unto you is born this day in the city of David a Savior, who is Christ the Lord. And this shall be a sign unto you: Ye shall find the babe wrapped in swaddling clothes, lying in a manger. And suddenly there was with the angel a multitude of the heavenly host praising God and saying, 'Glory to God in the highest, and on earth peace, good will toward men.'" (Luke 2:10-14 KJV)

Carols sung by angels in the early morn,
Honoring an infant in a stable born:
Round a lowly manger shepherds bow in awe—
Immortal is that picture, and without a flaw!
Songs of glad rejoicing, thus the day began
Tidings of salvation! God and Son of man
Move the heavenly chorus down to bless the earth.
Angels voice hosannas at our Savior's birth:
Singing of glad tidings, heaven stoops to earth.

Glory to the Father! Christ is born to reign!
Reverently the angels sound this glad refrain.
Earth, art thou rejoicing in the Prince of Peace?
Echo heaven's greetings! Jesus must increase
Til all earth and heaven glorifies His name.
Invoke God's blessing, and His praise proclaim!
Name the name of Jesus; He alone is best!
God so loved His people that He gave His best!
Sing and glorify Him, Jesus Christ is blest!

"Behold a virgin shall conceive, and bear a son, and shall call his name Immanuel." (Isaiah 7:14 KJV)

83 ~ II

"Thou shalt call his name JESUS: for he shall save his people from their sins." (Matthew 1:21 KJV)

If we had lived in that far day
Would we have laid Him on the hay?
We say, If we were living there
We would have given tender care
    To Jesus.

Oh what a joy it would have been
To welcome Jesus Christ within
Our home, and bid Him ever stay—
Yet, do we prove our faith today
    In Jesus.

We must receive the Holy Prince
Who came from heaven to convince
Our souls of God's eternal love—
A precious Gift from God above
    Is Jesus!

Dear God, we thank Thee for Thy Gift!
In humble gratitude we lift
Our ceaseless praise. Our souls proclaim
Hosannas to the holy name
    Of Jesus.

"For unto us a child is born, unto us a son is given: and the government shall be upon his shoulder: and his name shall be called Wonderful, Counsellor, The Mighty God, The Everlasting Father, The Prince of

Peace. Of the increase of his government and peace there shall be no end, upon the throne of David, and upon his kingdom, to order it, and to establish it with judgment and with justice from henceforth even forever. The zeal of the Lord of hosts will perform his." (Isaiah 9:6-7KJV)

84 ~ III

"Happy is the man that findeth wisdom, and the man that getteth understanding. For the merchandise of it is better than the merchandise of silver, and the gain thereof than fine gold. She is more precious than rubies: and all the things thou canst desire are not to be compared unto her." (Proverbs 3:13-15 KJV)

"Give instruction to a wise man, and he will be yet wiser; teach a just man, and he will increase in learning. The fear of the Lord is the beginning of wisdom: and the knowledge of the holy is understanding." (Proverbs 9:9-10 KJV)

If you, and I, had lived back there
Would we have been wise enough to share
The wise men's hope? Would we have gone
Faithfully journeying on—and on—
Over the desert to lands afar?
Would we have followed that guiding star?

Would we have thrilled with glad surprise
As we gazed into those shining eyes—
Forgetting our quest of weary miles
In the benediction of His smiles?
Today, are we finding what blessings are
Still hidden in prophecy's guiding star?

Would we have worshipped our Lord and King
With the choicest gifts which we could bring,
As we knelt, at last, in that far land
Gently to kiss His tiny hand?

Dare we to travel too swiftly in plane, or car,
To follow the Light of the Guiding Star?
Wise men never fail to find Jesus,
because, finding Jesus Christ is wisdom!

85 ~ END OF THE YEAR

RUBY TOBEY

Lord, thank You for these,
the year's memories,
and the things that made life worthwhile.
And for every hour,
and every wildflower,
You placed within my memory file.

Now, in the new year,
Lord, will You be near;
will You send what I need to grow?
I want to be kind
so fill up my mind
with ways I can let my love show.

For all my friends too,
I do pray that You
will help them this year through each day.
Give help in sorrow,
hope for tomorrow,
and joy as they go on their way.

Hotlinks
For More
Christmas Blessings
(Public Domain Sources)

"For God so loved the world that He gave His only Son, that whoever believes in Him should not perish but have eternal life."

(John 3:16)

READER AND LISTENER RESOURCES

Author/Educator/Clergyman Henry Van Dyke (1852-1933) has many writings now in "public domain." Several were popular throughout the year and became theatrical productions. Some of his writing is based on facts and some, because he was a novelist, are fanciful. Regardless of how time is spent during the "Christmas season," we've compiled a few "listening" options we hope you might like hearing. The first four are recordings of Van Dyke's Christmas thoughts:

86 ~A DREAM STORY: THE CHRISTMAS ANGEL

https://archive.org/details/spirit_of_christmas_jm_librivox/spirit ofxmas_01_vandyke.mp3

87 ~ A LITTLE ESSAY: CHRISTMAS GIVING AND CHRISTMAS LIVING

https://archive.org/details/spirit_of_christmas_jm_librivox/spirit ofxmas_02_vandyke.mp3

88 ~ A SHORT CHRISTMAS SERMON: KEEPING CHRISTMAS

https://archive.org/details/spirit_of_christmas_jm_librivox/spirit ofxmas_03_vandyke.mp3

89 ~ TWO CHRISTMAS PRAYERS

https://archive.org/details/spirit_of_christmas_jm_librivox/spirit ofxmas_04_vandyke.mp3

Two online resources, Biblegateway and Faithlife Bible, offer both written and audio options for the entire Bible. Faithlife Bible has study resources built into the free downloads. Here, though, are specific parts of the Christmas story through Biblegateway. For this particular book, we've chosen the *New Living Translation,* but you may select the version of your choice on the site.

90 ~ ANGEL'S VISIT TO MARY FROM LUKE 1
https://www.biblegateway.com/passage/?search=Luke+1&version=NLT

91 ~ MARY'S VISIT TO COUSIN ELIZABETH
https://www.biblegateway.com/passage/?search=Luke+1&version=NLT

92 ~ ANGEL'S VISIT TO JOSEPH
https://www.biblegateway.com/passage/?search=Matthew+1&version=NLT

93 ~ MARY AND JOSEPH GO TO BETHLEHEM
https://www.biblegateway.com/passage/?search=Luke+2&version=NLT

94 ~ ANGELS PROCLAIM BIRTH OF JESUS TO SHEPHERDS
https://www.biblegateway.com/passage/?search=Luke+2&version=NLT

95 ~ SHEPHERDS VISIT AND BECOME MISSIONARIES
https://www.biblegateway.com/passage/?search=Luke+2&version=NLT

96 ~ WISEMEN FOLLOW THE STAR TO JERUSALEM
https://www.biblegateway.com/passage/?search=Matthew+2&version=NLT

97 ~ MARY, JOSEPH, AND BABY JESUS FLEE TO EGYPT
https://www.biblegateway.com/passage/?search=Matthew+2&version=NLT

98 ~ HE LIVED AMONG US (LIFE OF CHRIST VIDEO FROM VOICE OF THE MARTYRS); (In 15 languages)
https://www.youtube.com/watch?v=O5KETYJJnIE _

99 ~ ON YOUTUBE WATCH: MATTHEW VIDEO POSTED BY TWO PREACHERS https://www.youtube.com/watch?v=h0qGrVcz-eQ

100 ~ THE JESUS MOVIE FOR KIDS –on YouTube:
https://www.youtube.com/watch?v=d-fsT6-nIOY

Biographies

of

Contributors

"Let the message about Christ, in all its richness, fill your lives. Teach and counsel each other with all the wisdom He gives. Sing psalms and hymns and spiritual songs to God with thankful hearts. And whatever you do or say, do it as a representative of the Lord Jesus, giving thanks through Him to God the Father."

(Colossians 3:17-18 NLT)

CONTRIBUTORS
IN ALPHABETICAL ORDER

Artist, educator, and state licensed producer, **Anna Lisa Alvarado** actively seeks to honor the Lord with her time and talents. She claims she left part of her heart in Belgium during one the most difficult stages of her life. She's the proud mom of two adult children and loves their expanding families.

John Anderson was born in Arizona and now lives in Oklahoma. He's married with two grown children. John wrote technical materials before his nonfiction submission, "Christmas Magic."

Former elementary teacher **Marilyn Boone** combined history, mystery, and romance in her first two novels in the young adult inspirational Legacy series; "Heartstrings" and "Becoming Rose" are on Amazon. She's also published by "Chicken Soup for the Soul" (Reboot Your Life). She enjoys many creative and musical activities, including playing her hammered dulcimer. Contact her via **marilyn.p.boone@gmail.com or www.marilynboone.com**

Cathy Bryant enjoys spinning heart-stirring stories of God's life-changing grace. Her first novel, "Texas Roads," was a 2009 American Christian Fiction Writers' Genesis contest finalist. Since then, she's added six novels to the beloved and best-selling Miller's Creek series, a Christmas novella, two Bible studies, and three devotional books. When not writing, you'll find her wrangling chickens and rabbits, rummaging through thrift stores, or up to her elbows in yet another home improvement project. She and her husband live in Arkansas' lovely Ozark Mountains near the world's cutest grandkids. Find out more about Cathy and her books at **https://CathyBryantBooks.wordpress.com**

Award-winner **Dr. Jeanetta Chrystie** enjoys the writing process. She has published over 800 articles in magazines, including *Christian History, Discipleship Journal, Mature Years, Church Libraries,* and *Clubhouse.* She's written 150+ columns for the *Northwest Christian Examiner/Times/Journal,* 85+ newsletter articles, and her 50+ poems and 100+ devotionals are in various books including "Short Stories Too" and college textbooks. She founded **www.OzarksACW.org**. Her website is: **www.ClearGlassView.com**.

Georgia and Harold Clark live in Stanton, Iowa, where they remain active members of their church and community. Earlier both were educators; Harold coached and became a principal and Georgia taught home economics. Now Harold keeps busy with part-time work and Georgia keeps the coffeepot on for friends. They have two adult children and one almost grown granddaughter whose activities keep the Clarks young. They enjoy camping, especially at beautiful Viking State Park near Stanton.

About twenty-five years ago **Bonnie Clarkson** began writing poems, devotions, short stories, object lessons, and plays. Bonnie says, "When I write, the endings surprise me and I usually learn a lesson from it." Bonnie has several Christmas plays that churches may want to use this year or in the Christmases to come. To contact her, please email her at: **bonnieclarkson3@gmail.com**

If you want to put together quick meals, **Cathey Cook's** "Simple Cooking" is a good resource. You'll find more recipes and interesting articles on her **https://catheycook.com** website. Cathey and Bill had their daughters mostly raised before Cathey started college, earned her Master's, and taught for several years. Recently she volunteered to teach homeschoolers in a couple subjects and she's begun research for more books. She's also a grandmother, a gardener, teaches Bible class on Sundays, plus helps provide music for worship services.

Memoir author **Sybil Copeland** writes to leave a legacy for her family, partly because the genealogy record-keeping stopped when she, as one of the set of identical triplets, arrived. Sybil contributes articles to her former hometown *Hominy News Progress,* and has had several stories published in Bartlesville (Oklahoma) WordWeavers' anthologies. Sybil is active in her church. She enjoys times with her family, including their adventures at fall deer camps and spring fishing trips.

Dianne Cox was a stay-at home mom for twenty-one years before taking on the challenge of working with computers. While working full-time, she attended night classes and obtained her CPS (Certified Professional Secretary) and, thirty-six years after high school graduation, an Associates Degree in Business Administration. She's the proud mother of four, grandmother to seven and has two great-grandchildren. "And Jesus Smiled" is her first attempt at writing, which she thoroughly enjoyed and hopes to continue. Dianne currently resides in Oklahoma.

Helping people overcome their difficult pasts is one of **Mary DeMuth's** many gifts, in addition to authoring over 30 books and hosting international "Restory" events plus over four seasons of "Restory" podcasts. Mary is a wife and mother, an international speaker, a workshop leader, and a former church planter. Some of Mary's tips include: make integrity your choice, serve the person in front of you, pray with friends, call that frustrated child, this world is about serving, do unnoticed things with joy, and count your blessings when things don't go your way. Find this Texan's books on her website or on Amazon at **https://www.amazon.com/Mary-E.-DeMuth/e/B001HD2X7W** and catch fascinating "Restory" interviews at **http://www.marydemuth.com/restory-show-inventory/**.

Harriett Ford is an author and a long-time reporter and humor columnist with recurring dreams about conversations with Chief Speaking Bull who is, of course, related to Chief Standing Bull and Sitting Bull. Harriett is a Faithwriters International devotional writer, Stonecroft Ministries inspirational speaker, and a supporter of Jacob's House (Jacobshouse.org). Her latest nonfiction book is "Supervention" which includes life-changing experiences. Find more about Harriett at facebook.com/harriettbarnettford, on Amazon at **https://www.amazon.com/Harriett-Ford/e/B001K8X4Z4 or at harriettford.blogspot.com**

Rosamary Gilligan lives on a farm in southeast Kansas with her husband and four youngest of their 13 children. Her previous writing includes Vacation Bible School curriculums and programs, 4-H skits, and dramas for teens. Rosamary is currently working on personalized stories for her 22 grandchildren. She enjoys life and loves people! She also loves testifying about God's faithfulness to her family in word and song (the whole family is musically gifted) and helping others discover how to know the peace she has in Him!

Barbara Gordon began freelance writing when she retired from public school teaching and administration. She writes articles for a monthly writers' group newsletter and has had several devotionals published in anthology books. She has also been published in *Live, The Secret Place, The Breakthrough Intercessor* and *Pray* magazines. Barbara lives in west-central Missouri with her husband of 41 years and enjoys family time with three sons, three daughters-in-law and six grandchildren.

Susan Haddan worked as a community college registrar and the accompanist for its choir before she began enjoying retirement in 2014. She and her husband farm in southeast Kansas and love to spend time with their two adult daughters and two grandchildren. Susan says her hobbies include anything she can create – gardening, giving new life to old furniture, and cooking, when she's not reading. For the past year, she's helped care for her 99 year-old mother. She feels God has blessed their family and answered many prayers. She and her husband attend

Savonburg Covenant Church where Susan has been the organist for 49 years.

William Cody Hall told us about his life in the story about his clever proposal to Emily. Cody and Emily met in 2013 while Cody was a summer intern at SonSet Solutions in Elkhart, Indiana. In 2016, Cody and Emily began dating and were married in May of 2017. They are full-time missionaries at SonSet Solutions, with Cody working as a mechanical engineer, and Emily working in the accounting department. To follow Cody and Emily's ministry through periodic updates, please contact them at **williamchall12@gmail.com.**

People in **Cassandra (Sandy) Jordan's** church and community take part in her Christmas plays to bring Christmas to life each year. Sandy says she never knows who will take which roles, so each year's characters bring variety to the plays and she keeps writing them. Sandy has a "Bits and Pieces" column, writes poetry, devotionals, both fiction and nonfiction materials, and is working on a historical romance series she plans to call "The Cherokee Rose." She's a busy person, but even so, some of Sandy's writing has been published by Dayspring cards and she also writes for the Nazarene's *Standard* publication.

DeAnna Kahre has worked as a personal secretary, as an Indian Education Tutor, and now helps manage rentals. She has attended Redeemer Lutheran Church in Bartlesville most of her life. She lives with her husband in rural Ramona, Oklahoma. DeAnna heard about the anthology through a workshop Margery Kisby Warder presented at the Washington County Fair in 2017 which included an invitation to write about Christmas for an upcoming book. We're glad she did. She continues to be active in her church programs.

Astrid Kisby, (1913-2010), the first American born child of her Swedish parents, sailed through school and taught five years before marrying her farmer sweetheart. When their children were self-sufficient, she supplemented income by working in a medical clinic. Her love of Jesus Christ kept her active in her church into her 90s when she agreed to move closer to her children who were concerned for her safety. She blessed many lives, treasured family and friends, and wrote over 100 poems now online in **"Astrid's Gift to Her Loved Ones."**

Kentucky is now home base for **Jim Kisby** and his wife because IBM moved them there several years ago. Uncle Sam interrupted Jim's employment with Martin Marietta before he began work for IBM, then Lexmark from which he retired at age 70. Since Jim's mind likes to be creative, his latest successful invention is a motorized precision blade sharpener for large mowers, which he crafted in his garage. With four grown children's families living in Florida and

Texas, the couple puts on lots of miles in a year's time, but almost all Christmases brought them back to Kansas while his parents were alive.

Loren and Judy Kisby live in Munden, Kansas, a community about 40 miles from where he grew up. Loren taught school before returning to farm and establishing his "Rogue Hoe Manufacturing" business in Munden. He has an interesting story about his own hand-made hoe that he kept picking off the burn pile for odd jobs before it hit him that others, too, might find it useful. Now he manufactures over 60 styles of popular steel tools. (To see what many claim is a "perfect" hoe and popular fire tools, go to **http://www.prohoe.com**) Loren was given an award for his 40 years of teaching and leadership roles at the Wesleyan Church in Belleville where Judy has also taught young children for many years. Judy worked as a librarian at Belleville Public Library, specializing in the children's reading program before her retirement. Judy's delicious Swedish foods became a traditional part of Christmas festivities.

Lori Klickman is active in her church in Grove, Oklahoma where she often has shared some of her devotional writing. She's hoping to have her first book published in the near future through an agent who is promoting her manuscript. Like most writers, she has a job that pays, and in her case, she's the office manager and multi-line sales representative at the Neil Jarvis State Farm Agency. If you read her writing, you know she has a "funny bone" while still writing truths. Watch for this author's book, hopefully in the near future.

Inspirational speaker, artist, teacher, and businesswoman **Penny Robichaux Koontz** has overcome obstacles most of her life because she believes she can make a difference in her family, church, business, and community. From Penny's triumphs, especially over two bouts with polio, she has coached others, nationally and internationally, to hurdle their obstacles, too. Newspapers and other media have featured her life's accomplishments, which included starting a homeless shelter in Texas and launching Jacob's House for at-risk children in Chestnut Ridge, Missouri. Her encouraging book, "I Thought You Had a Bigger Dream" is on Amazon at **https://www.amazon.com/Penny-Robichaux-Koontz/e/B005D938VG**. Jacob's House is a 501(c)3; for ways to brighten children's futures, go to **http://www.jacobshouse.org**.

Arnold Kropp was born and raised in Chicago. After high school, he tried college but without a sense of what his major should be, he enlisted in the Army. Witnessing the impact communism in East Germany had upon its people has influenced his life and his writing. His two books are "Montesquieu – New World Island" and "Montesquieu – New World Island Sequel" which are on

Amazon at https://www.amazon.com/Arnold-R.-Kropp/e/B00AL2MPDM.

Instructor **Jane Landreth's** fingers likely flew across computer keys while you read this Christmas book. Publishers eagerly swooped up her Bible curriculum and over 3,000 stories, as well as countless articles, games, puzzles, and other materials to enrich religious magazines. She's written six Bible storybooks, co-authored seven creative idea books, and self-published one. Her writing has been translated into Russian, Romanian, Haitian, and Spanish. Public and private schools, and several colleges, asked Jane to teach writing. On three trips to Belarus, Jane taught church personnel how to write Bible curriculum for their students. Find her books at: **https://www.amazon.com/Jane-Landreth/e/B002FZIBEU**

Nate Lee was born and raised in Oklahoma. He graduated from Oklahoma State University with a degree in manufacturing engineering technology. He now lives in Kansas, where by day he works as an aircraft process engineer, but by night he is an avid player of video games, lover of music (he's a mediocre drummer), and affectionate husband and father of four. His debut spiritual warfare thriller, "Imposter," is available wherever fine books are sold or on Amazon at **https://www.amazon.com/Imposter-Nate-Lee/dp/1"277863X/ref** Find more information at **authornatelee.com.**

Janis Lussmyer is a self-published author of two books: a memoir, *Three Corners Has My Cat: Caregiving in Alzheimer's Time,* and a devotional, *Random Reflections.* Her next book will be released in late 2017. *When I Am Weak* records her journey through breast cancer. She lives in Bartlesville, Oklahoma. Janis' books are found at **https://www.amazon.com/Janis-Lussmyer/e/B00O6M15CK** and **https://www.amazon.com/Three-Corners-Has-Cat-Caregiving/dp/1494366428/ref**

Being with family brings a sparkle to **Sofi McCutcheon's** eyes. She loves animals, and animals quickly know they've found a loyal friend when they are with Sofi. Her sensory poem about Christmas was written as part of a school assignment a few years ago, and those who hear it tend to smile at the memories it triggers for them. Sofi has a few years of school ahead, but it's clear she will bless many lives with her enthusiasm for life and gifts of generosity and encouragement.

For years, Stanton, Iowa's fourth graders counted on **Karen Mead's** very capable and creative teaching to help them lock-in foundational skills both in and out of her classroom. Each year her students "adopted" a "grandparent" from the local nursing home through regular visits, which brought mutual joy to the children and the chosen residents. Even as a full-time teacher, Karen helped with the After-School Club and other activities at her church. She and her husband live on a farm south of Stanton where Karen's flowers bring a smile to those driving past. They enjoy their children's families visits to their farm.

Life brings changes, and recently for **Becky Mueller** that has meant setting aside her professional roles to help care for an elderly member of the family. Becky always has a ready smile and a genuine concern for those around her. She has worked in the school system, hosted tours to historical sites, and remains active in both children and teen ministry at her church and in the Stonecroft Ministries' women's programs in Bartlesville, Oklahoma.

Speaker, award-winning columnist and award-winning author **Jonita Mullins** lives and writes Oklahoman in her ten published books. In 2017, "The Jefferson Highway in Oklahoma" won Best Non-Fiction Book from the Oklahoma Writers Federation. Jonita's "Journey to an Untamed Land" recounts the work of missionaries and school teachers among Oklahoma's Osages, and two sequels are included in "The Missions of Indian Territory" series. Churches, civic groups, libraries, women's conferences, and others seeking a motivational or historical presentation have featured Jonita, who digs up Oklahoma history from her 100-year-old fixer-upper in Muskogee. She's also written about her first hometown in "Haskell: A Centennial Celebration." Find her books through her **okieheritage.com** website, in shops, or at **https://www.amazon.com/Jonita-Mullins/e/B00JUW1BJ8** to sharpen knowledge of Oklahoma's rich history.

Jean Nelson started "Smoking Kills" to encourage youth to live without the tobacco addiction that made her a widow eighteen years ago. For years, Jean's non-profit offered addiction education within Montgomery County (Iowa) schools, provided thousands of dollars in scholarships to college-bound tobacco-free seniors, and sponsored the "Smoking Kills" youth baseball team. Dwindling interest from students and coaches is resulting in legal dissolution of her nonprofit work. Now Jean spends more time singing in nursing homes and reading in the "oasis" her son-in-law provided that overlooks her rock and water garden. Jean hopes to write a cancer-survivor book but appreciated the opportunity to provide the shortened version in this anthology.

Pearl Pierson (*as told by her granddaughter, Mary Rooks*) My grandmother, Pearl Pierson, born in The Dalles, Oregon 1886, exemplified living faith. She opened their home for classes during early beginnings of San Jose Bible College. "Grandmother's Lullaby" and "ABC Book About Jesus" were penned to commemorate my birth in 1946. She was still writing music and attending classes when a heart attack took her life in 1955. My fondest memories are her kindness shown in teaching me to count, watching her build me a small table and chairs from scrap lumber, and holiday meals with cousins in her living room. *(Editor's note: Pearl Pierson's writing was featured in publications for churches for many years and her book, "Found" is reprinted online.)*

Matthew A. Poe humbly describes himself as "a child of God, who is a husband to his wife and a father to their daughter, both precious gifts from God." Matthew writes and edits trade magazines for his day job. He has dabbled in fiction on and off for years, but now is sharing more fiction, more "parables," like Jesus. He blogs about the Lord, about writing, about the outdoors, and whatever else is on his mind at **poesheart.blogspot.com.** You can also follow him on Twitter **@poesheart.** Watch for more from Matthew.

Pastor Haralan Popov pastored the largest Protestant church in Bulgaria. After the Communist occupation of Bulgaria, Pastor Popov spent 13 years and two months in sixteen different prisons and slave camps. Upon his release, he created a ministry to the Persecuted Church known as Evangelism to Communist Lands, now known as *Door of Hope International,* located in Glendale, California (**http://www.dohi.org**). Pastor Popov died November 14, 1988. The ministry continues under the direction of his son, Paul Popov. His book, "Tortured for His Faith" is on Kindle at **https://www.amazon.com/dp/B005DHYCBI.**

Doug Quinn and his wife Penny have lived in Bartlesville for almost fifty years during which time Penny taught and Doug worked at Phillips Petroleum. Now Penny volunteers for several ministries. Doug is the Board of Directors president for **The Journey Home**, which came out of Doug's meetings with medical personnel after he'd volunteered to give palliative care through Jane Phillips Medical Center. Aware terminally ill patients were sometimes without families or funds for care in their final days, Doug drew up a business plan to care for life's "weary travelers." **The Journey Home** now has a waiting list after serving over 300 patients without cost to the patient or the families. Tax-deductible donations can be given at **thejourneyhomeok.com** or by calling 918.876.4184. The Quinns are active in Grace Community Church. Devotionals written by Doug appear in *Upper Room* and he's recently begun nurturing his interest in writing fiction.

Carla (Olson) Rydberg and her husband live - and work - on a farm in Iowa, and include among the wonderful blessings in their lives their children, 14 grandkids and 5 greats! Her deep desire is to have a teachable heart and be an encourager, pointing people to Jesus who loves us with an amazing, everlasting love. Though she wouldn't say so, Carla is also known for her magazine-cover worthy desserts and baked goods, especially at Christmastime.

Marilyn Seymour's career was mostly in Home Health after earning her R.N. from Wichita's Wesley School of Nursing. She interrupted her career to raise three sons and followed her husband's employment obligations to several states. After a few winters trying to stay upright on icy paths into patients' homes in Connecticut, where she was awarded "Nurse of the Year" by the nursing agency, she traded snow shovels for sunshine and retired in Florida. Marilyn is active in her church but also volunteers with the Salvation Army's ministries to the elderly and homeless individuals. In her free time reads several books a week.

Sally U. Smith founded a newspaper for her junior high friends using a manual typewriter and lots of carbon paper. Subsequently, Sally's later writing includes over 500 articles for newspapers, magazines, newsletters, and online publications. She contributed devotionals and stories to *Cup Of Comfort Devotional For Mothers*, *Along The Way For Teens, Extraordinary Answers To Prayers,* and *101 Facets Of Faith.* Her first book in her "Pray to Win" series, "Pit Crew: Praying For Our Pastors To Finish The Race," will be released May 8, 2018. You can reach her at: **newbeginning.sally@gmail.com**

The elderly have had a dedicated friend in **Mary Ruth Steger** ever since the days when she accompanied her pastor father on congregational visits. After she grew up and married, Mary Ruth raised their children and began working as an activity coordinator at their local care center in South Dakota. When her husband retired from farming, the couple moved to be near their daughter's family in Oklahoma and Mary Ruth was hired to provide activities and Bible studies for Green Country Village Retirement Community, even when she was well into her senior years. She retired after a hospitalization in 2017. Mary Ruth and her husband are active in their church and also frequently host "Skip-Bo" and "Pegs and Jokers" game times for friends and neighbors. Keeping track of their active grandchildren is joy for them, too

Kevin Talton is a third generation mariner holding a 1600 Ton Masters License issued by the United States Coast Guard. His father, grandfather, and uncle all taught him how to fish and operate boats at a very young age. One of his passions as a Christian is to explore God's creation through outdoor activities such as hiking, scuba diving, and nature photography. Kevin also enjoys the art of wood-burning (pyrography), and creating bonsai landscapes (Penjing), which are sometimes made available at art and craft fairs. Kevin has a **Christian blog entitled "And God Created..."** readers may enjoy. Often Kevin's social media photos taken from "his office" are water scenes with breathtaking sunrises and sunsets. When his feet are on land, he resides in Central Virginia with his beautiful wife and young son.

Scribbles and Sketches is the free newsletter **Ruby Tobey** has mailed to her loyal readers for many years. Each edition includes ink sketches of nature or rural scenes so pleasant to the eye. Ruby lives at 2305 West 32nd Street South in Wichita (67217), which is the address to use if you would like to ask her to include you on her mailing list. Ruby designs a 5 and ½ by 11-inch calendar with sketches and poetry; it sells for just $2. She has painted on porcelain and china and also makes jewelry. The publishers of her **"Thoughts and Prayers from the Scribbles & Sketches Studio" and "Scribbles and Sketches, Volume II"** books went out of business so it may be best to purchase them directly from Ruby. Her Internet shop is: **Etsy.com/shop/ScribblesSketches.**

Margery Kisby Warder just can't seem to get away from "all things writing," especially now that the children have families of their own, though she welcomes opportunities to be with family and friends. Her passion is to write and encourage other Christian writers, sometimes by hosting "Missional" Christian Writers© retreats and workshops. In 2017, two of her "one syllable" essays were published in Susan King's "Short and Sweet" and "Short and Sweet Too" books. Margery's humor and poetry won awards in 2016 and 2017, including a Mount Hermon Christian Writers Conference scholarship. She recently began combining her scripture-based poetry with art or photography on canvas. Follow her on Amazon, Facebook or through her website blog on **margerywarder.wordpress.com.** Several of her books are online at **https://www.amazon.com/Margery-Kisby-Warder/e/B00GPELE7I**

Paul Warder spent most of his adult life pastoring churches in Wisconsin, Indiana, Kansas, and Iowa. At one point, he was a teacher and principal at a Christian school in Texas. Now retired, he has co-authored two devotional books, occasionally preaches or portrays Biblical characters for congregations, and speaks in behalf of persecuted Christians through his volunteer work with The Voice of the Martyrs (**https://www.persecution.com**). He and Margery host "Missional" Christian Writers workshops and retreats and he encourages Margery's ministry because, he says, since she supported his pastoral ministry for their first forty years of marriage it's his turn to support hers. They make their home in Bartlesville where they are involved in Bible studies and other ministries when they're not traipsing off to visit their children's families.

When **T. R. Hobbs-York** learned what a pencil could do, she fell in love with writing creatively. She says she's a simple country/small town woman who loves the Lord with all of her heart and hopes to share Him, His love, mercy, grace and salvation, in her poetry and stories. Tawnya says she's not a perfect Christian yet, but she strives to be a light for God every day in whatever role she has for the day. She is sometimes the friendly face meeting customers checking out at Walmart and she values time with family and friends. T. R. Hobbs-York plans on having her first book, "FROM THE CRADLE TO THE CROSS: God's Promise Fulfilled" finished by the end of November 2017. **Watch for it on Amazon**.

*Remember, dear readers, two words about one
of the authors' work is sometimes enough encouragement
to keep them writing.
If you make a comment about
"Celebrating Christmas"
on Amazon or Facebook, it will be much appreciated.
You are welcome to mention your favorite submissions.
Thank you in behalf of all 45 individuals
who submitted to this anthology
and those who helped with its publication.*

ABOUT THE EDITOR/COMPILER

Margery Kisby Warder encourages other Christian writers to get their work out of the drawers or off their hard drives and polish them so they are ready for readers. When she suggests changes, she doesn't claim to be an expert; she strives to keep the writer's voice but to spare them embarrassment. She's seen errors in her own published works, too, and endorses the wisdom of the more experienced who say every book, except the Lord's, will have errors and cause debates about technicalities. Bottom line, she hopes writers she coaches do the best they can with the time they can allot to a project. She suspects most of us will go to our graves wishing we could edit or rewrite our lives a bit more, too, which makes her extremely grateful Jesus offers to cover mankind's messes with His righteousness.

Readers will notice writer's voices varied within this Christmas collection. As the editor, Margery hopes the final decisions about fragments and commas seem purposeful, or better yet, go unnoticed by the wide range of readers who enjoy this book…and that typos fled. ☺

In 2015 Margery began "Missional" Christian Writers after authors told of their boxes of books and the huge debts they'd incurred after signing contracts with "publishing companies." She applauds the 2 percent of writers who can live off their earnings and whose work delights not only readers, but agents and publishing houses, too. However, since most writers have financial obligations but still want to offer their writing to readers while without depleting resources they intended to use elsewhere in God's kingdom work, Margery tries to offer encouragement and opportunities. As a Christian author and speaker, Margery believes she is accountable for her words, whether written or spoken. If you agree and have a story but not many resources, you might want to attend Margery's retreats or workshops. Contact her at **author.speaker4Him@gmail.com**.

Margery loves her role as a wife, thinks her most creative efforts were required in being a mom, and she is delighted to have grandchildren to fuss over when the miles can be ignored. Oh, and yes, she does have a writer dog; this one doesn't stay up as late as the last one, but this writer dog's excuse is that she's going in to start warming the bed.

*Margery's on Facebook, has a blog, and about a dozen of her books are on Amazon at **https://www.amazon.com/Margery-Kisby-Warder/e/B00GPELE7I** or other places online.*

TIPS TO RECEIVE JESUS CHRIST AS SAVIOR (RSV Bible)

Think on this: God loves us. He wants us to spend eternity in His presence. He is Holy. Sin cannot be part of heaven. Sin has to be punished: either by us or through loving God's only provision: Jesus Christ. God offered His sinless Holy Son to be the Lamb sacrificed for our sins. Jesus died and rose again in order for sin's debt to be paid for any who would receive Him as Savior and Lord, any who believe in Him. Salvation is a gift. As with any gift, it has to be received to become our own.

HOW CAN THIS FREE GIFT BE OURS?
ANY OF US MAY CHOOSE TO BE SAVED

Admit we have not let God rule our lives. We mess up both intentionally and unintentionally. Godly repentance leads to sorrow over our sins. Good news: Jesus died to save us from eternal death if we trust/believe Jesus Christ to be our Savior.

Believe Jesus Christ was sent by God to save the "world" *(John 3:16-17: "For God so loved the world (individuals) that He gave His only Son (Jesus), that whoever (anyone, anywhere, anytime) believes in Him should not perish (head into an eternity without God's favor) but have eternal life. For God sent His Son...that the world might be saved through Him.")*

Jesus shed His blood for all people's sins. He was virgin born, lived, was crucified, buried, and rose from death to the life eternal He wants us to also have. Now He, only Jesus, makes things right between us and our just God when we believe in Jesus as Savior.

If we refuse Jesus, what then? We spend eternity apart from God.

God's Word tell us that none of us can earn heaven or God's favor: *"For by grace (unearned favor) have you been saved through faith; and this is not your own doing, it is the gift of God, not because of works lest any man should boast." (Ephesians 2:8-9)*

If we repent and receive Jesus as our Savior, we are receiving the FREE gift of salvation from God. Ought we not thank Jesus for dying to pay for our sinfulness, for dying to make peace between God and us? We can invite Him to come and live within us as our new King. Read on –

*John 1:12: ..**to all** who received Him/Jesus, **(to all)** who believed in His name, He gave power to become children of God, who were born not of blood nor of the will of the flesh nor of the will of man, but of God.*

Prayer is talking to a loving God, telling Him what is on your heart. There is no exact words to pray, so talk with Him on your own unless you want to consider the suggested prayer below. God listens.

A SUGGESTED PRAYER IF YOU WANT
TO JOIN GOD'S FOREVER FAMILY:

Heavenly Father, I don't deserve to become part of Your family, but I ask You to receive me because I believe Your Holy Son, Jesus Christ, died on the cross to pay all the penalties for my sin. I know I am unclean and unholy, but I now ask to receive Jesus as my only Savior and Lord. Help me follow Jesus faithfully all the remaining days of my life. Help me rely upon the truths in the Bible and upon guidance from Your Holy Spirit who now lives within me because I want my life to honor You.
In Jesus' Name, Amen.

If you prayed to receive Jesus Christ as your Savior and Lord, our prayer is that you study God's Word (free copies are online) and also find a group of Christ's followers who study and discuss the Holy Bible. We know not everyone has a Bible or knows other Christ-followers, so we pray that your loving Heavenly Father will teach you through people and resources He brings into your life. Others are praying for you. Now you can pray for Christ's followers, too.

Made in the USA
Columbia, SC
27 November 2017